Mike and Janya,

We hope you
are enjoying your
cruise experience.

Dean and Sharon

Algrove Publishing Limited
36 Mill Street, P.O. Box 1238, Almonte, Ontario, Canada K0A 1A0
Telephone: (613) 256-0350   Fax: (613) 256-0360   Email: sales@algrove.com

Cover Image: *This photo was taken, circa 1912, on board the barque
Imperator Aleksander II (ex. Grassendale) built in Workington, UK in 1885.
The photographer was Captain Victor Albert Henriksson (1869-1947).
We thank Captain Hannu A. Vartiainen of the Rauma Maritime Museum,
Finland, for his assistance in acquiring this photo for the cover.*

Copyright Rauma Maritime Museum (Kalle and Jussi Aarnio Collection)

*To see more photos from this collection go to the Rauma Maritime Museum,
Finland website: www.rmm.fi/english/museum/index.htm*

Library and Archives Canada Cataloguing in Publication

Davis, Charles G. (Charles Gerard), 1870-1959
    How sails are made and handled : with a chapter on racing kinks / by Charles G.
Davis.

(Classic reprint series)
Reprint. First published: New York : Rudder Pub. Co., 1922.
ISBN 1-897030-43-6

    1. Sails. 2. Sailing. I. Title. II. Series: Classic reprint series (Almonte, Ont.)

VM532.D38 2005   623.8'62   C2005-906024-7

Printed in Canada
#1-4-06

Publisher's Note

The various books Charles Davis wrote over the years are based on a wealth of experience. However, he was not infallible; he would have benefited from a good editor. It may be some 76 years late but this book has now had the benefit of a good edit, the kind that only winnows out the chaff and small stones, leaving behind all the grains of truth. If that same good editor (Robert Lee of Calgary) saw this note, he would probably have suggested avoiding the florid prose of the previous sentence. But he didn't.

Leonard G. Lee, Publisher
Almonte, Ontario
April 2006

How We Make Our Books - *You may not have noticed, but this book is quite different from other softcover books you might own. The vast majority of paperbacks, whether mass-market or the more expensive trade paperbacks, have the pages sheared and notched at the spine so that they may be glued together. The paper itself is often of newsprint quality. Over time, the paper will brown and the spine will crack if flexed. Eventually the pages fall out.*

All of our softcover books, like our hardcover books, have sewn bindings. The pages are sewn in signatures of sixteen or thirty-two pages and these signatures are then sewn to each other. They are also glued at the back but the glue is used primarily to hold the cover on, not to hold the pages together.

We also use only acid-free paper in our books. This paper does not yellow over time. A century from now, this book will have paper of its original color and an intact binding, unless it has been exposed to fire, water, or other catastrophe.

There is one more thing you will note about this book as you read it; it opens easily and does not require constant hand pressure to keep it open. In all but the smallest sizes, our books will also lie open on a table, something that a book bound only with glue will never do unless you have broken its spine.

The cost of these extras is well below their value and while we do not expect a medal for incorporating them, we did want you to notice them.

How Sails Are Made and Handled

With a Chapter on Racing Kinks

BY

CHARLES G. DAVIS

1922

Algrove Publishing
Classic Reprint Series

Foreword

TO those yachtsmen who have a fondness for wind jamming this book on sails by Charles G. Davis will be not only of interest but of great value. Mr. Davis is not only a practical sailor but he is also a student and he knows theoretically about the rules that govern sailing and sailmaking, and he knows practically how to obtain the best results from all rules and theories.

The name of Charles G. Davis is a household word wherever there is a sailing vessel. He began at first to handle small craft and then having thoroughly mastered the rudiments, he studied Naval Architecture and designing and paid particular attention to sails. He has made long ocean voyages in sailing vessels purely for the love of sailing and the experience it gave him and then he settled down at home to build vessels and to superintend their construction.

With him sailing has become a hobby, not to be taken up and dropped at odd times but that he might learn all he could and by writing about what he learned help others who love sailing. This book may consequently be regarded as authoritative. Many of its chapters have been already published in THE RUDDER but there has been such a demand for a work on this subject that the articles have been collected and put in book form together with some additional matter from Mr. Davis's pen. Among the subjects treated are the sails of many different rigs found in all parts of the world; materials used in the manufacture of the canvas; the proper shape of jibs and how they should be handled and trimmed; the action of the wind; center of effort area and shape of mainsails; relation of spars to the shapes of the sails and then some useful hints about the care of sails and some racing kinks. The book is well illustrated with pictures drawn by Mr. Davis who can show in a picture what it is often hard to explain in words.

Contents

Sails 7

Sail and Rig Variations, Materials Used for Sails, etc.. 7

How Sails Are Made........................... 47

Center of Effort, Area and Shape of Mainsails 67

Proper Shape and Trimming for Jibs............ 86

Action of the Wind........................... 98

Sail Shape and Other Factors 106

Getting the Proper Set to the Sail................ 125

Storing Sails 136

Racing Kinks 140

A Typical Marconi Rig.

6

- Sails -
l and Rig Variations,
ials Used for Sails, etc.

to have been neglected, for some rea-
er, by those historians and writers on
who have handed down to us descrip-
sels of past ages.

To them the ship alone seemed worthy of description. Perhaps this was because they knew, from having seen ships built, how the hull was put together and
for that reason they took more interest in describing
that with which they were familiar. Few men, outside
of sailmakers, who have worked on the bench, have
ever seen the complete process of making a sail.

Then, too, ships' sails were generally made in a
loft that, as a rule, was in some unpretentious and
out-of-the-way spot. For sailmakers needed floor
space whereon to spread their canvas while their profits prohibited any elaborate display or costly rentals.
One might walk under or around a sail-loft many
times and never know such an industry was being carried on overhead in the barn-like building.

A description of a steamship today describes in
minute detail her engine and the propeller wheel, the
medium through which the rotary motion of her en-
gines is converted into forward motion to the ship.
The propeller is of a fixed metal shape that can be
described by exact angles, but a ship's sail, while it,
too, is the medium supplying the push that sends the
ship ahead, is one of a flexible material and of varying
angles and curves.

7

The very complexity of the problem makes it all the more interesting. How little we know of ancient sails and of exact dates as to when sails were first made and of what materials.

It is to awaken a keener interest in sails and to give

Native Boat on Lake Chapala, Mexico

to yachtsmen some points on the use of the sails of today these articles have been written.

According to the dictionary, *sail* is a piece of canvas cloth or fabric of some kind spread to the wind to cause or assist in causing a vessel to move through the water.

Dædalus, of Athens, is accredited with the invention of the mast and sail and the year given as 1240 B. C. Canvas is spoken of as a coarse cloth, made of hemp

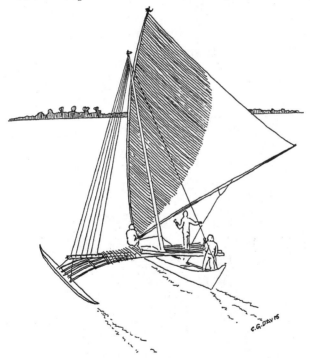

Marshall Island Canoe with Grass Matting Sail

or flax, while in an old English encyclopedia, sail cloth is mentioned as a very strong fabric, woven generally with linen yarns; but in America it has been made wholly of cotton, and in this country (England) under Armitage's patent, of cotton and linen mixed.

A Burmese Boat

10

When the schooner yacht America won the America's Cup in 1851, the English boats did have sails made of flax, while the America's sails were made of cotton and the superiority in the set of her sails, they standing much flatter than the English boats' baggy sails, is a matter of history.

A "Stackie" or Thames River Hay Barge

In foreign countries many different kinds of sails were and still are used, both as regards to their shape and the material of which they are made.

Grass and bamboo matting is used for the making of sails in the Far East, the Malay lorchas and Marshall

An Italian Felucca

Island canoes using the leaves of the screw pine. In New Zealand the rampo rush is used and the Eskimo uses the intestines of the walrus to make sails of. These and the sails of the Arab dhow, where each seam is roped, making a surface that is full of ridges, and the Chinese grass matting sails with bamboo battens, are to us, curiosities.

It is to be regretted that more specific details on sails have not been preserved by ancient writers on maritime matters. The ships themselves are described at length, their shape, size, construction and much of their fittings, as if the ship were the man, the sails merely the clothes he wore. This is true in one way of looking at it, and yet we hear many today remark, "It's the clothes that make the man."

This is truer, perhaps, in the ship's case than in the man's for the sails, good or bad, exert a far greater influence in the making of a boat's reputation than most men are aware of.

All that we have from the past are pictures drawn from imagination, prompted by what few facts historians have handed down to us, showing galleys of various shapes with one or more squaresails decorated like pieces of tapestry.

The crude figures of three huge lions decorated the sail on the king's own ship in King Richard's time, and the sails on the Greek galleys in the eleventh century, B. C., were colored sometimes in stripes, sometimes solid red, while the sails of the royal craft were dyed purple, a color always associated with royalty.

These sails were made of linen or grass cloth, and

bound with hide, the skins of seals and hyenas being considered as charms to ward off lightning

The word cotton is derived from the Arabic *gatn, kotan* or *kutn,* signifying soft. When Egypt was in her glory she had her own cotton industries and India was famous for the cotton tissues it produced When the early explorers landed in the new world, they found the

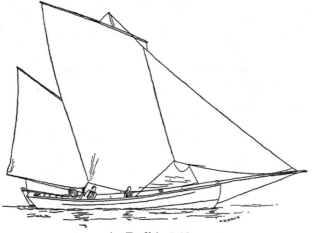

An English Coble

Aztecs of Mexico and the Incas of Peru were also well versed in the weaving of cotton cloths.

Beverly, Mass., may be called the birthplace of the cotton industry in the United States. The Beverly Company, founded in 1787, built a small brick factory on Bass River for the manufacture of cotton cloth, but they met with many difficulties and were not successful.

In England at that time, cotton weaving was being successfully carried on, Mr. John Wyatt having made the first attempt at cotton spinning in 1730 and in 1738 invented spinning by machinery. But the English Government jealously guarded the secrets of this business and her customs officers seized and forbade the exporting

A Ketch

of any cotton-weaving machines to the colonies, a law to that effect having been passed in 1773.

It was not until an Englishman, named Samuel Slater, who emigrated to America in 1789, and who built from memory a loom such as was then in use in England for the old Quaker firm of Almy & Brown at Pawtucket, R. I., completing it December 20, 1790 that the cotton industry really started in this country.

Experiments in cotton spinning machinery were being made not only in Massachusetts, but in many other states along the coast. In 1792, Eli Whitney, graduating from

Saint Malo Luggers

college at New Haven, Conn., went to Georgia, and in 1793, invented the saw gin for removing the seed from the cotton fibre; this gave a great impetus to the cotton-weaving business—it started industries in Philadelphia, and in 1822 we are told, cotton was first woven into sail cloth at Paterson, N. J.

We read how the first yacht ever launched in the United States was the Onrust, a decked craft 44¼ feet long on deck, of 11 feet breadth, built by Adrian Blok on the bank of the Hudson River, on Manhattan Island from trees cut on the island in the Summer of 1614.

Blok had been sent out by the merchants of Amster-

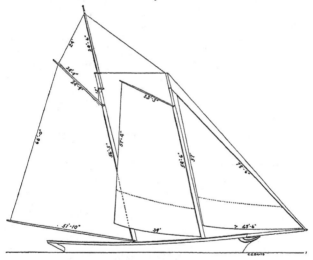

Original Sail Plan of America

dam as a trader, and in this small boat he explored the then unknown waters of Long Island Sound, then known as "The Devil's Belt," discovering and naming Block Island.

As sail cloth was not made in America in those days, where did Blok get his sails from? Evidently they were made from Holland duck and were the first sails made up for a boat in this country.

In 1633 a small ship was built at or near Boston, which was one of the first vessels of sea-going size constructed in New England. She undoubtedly also had sails made of the flax sail cloth made across the water.

As it was 1621 before the first experiment in cotton culture was made in Virginia, and 1790 when the first successful crop of Sea Island cotton was grown by Wm. Elliott on Hilton Head near Beaufort, S. C., though the year before, 1789, James Habersham exported the first bale of native-grown cotton to England, we may be sure these boats did not carry home-spun canvas.

New England merchants were doing a thriving business with India, China, and other Far Eastern countries as the records found in some old log-books show, along about 1759, or thereabouts.

Where their ships' sails came from there is nothing to show. That cotton formed part of the cargoes of vessels returning from Bombay, India, in 1784, and from the West Indies in 1788, there are documents to prove, but in all probabilities this cotton was used in the manufacture of home-spun clothing.

When Perry fitted out his fleet in 1812, at Erie, Pa., (at that time called Presque Isle) a number of sailmakers were sent out there from Philadelphia, to cut out and sew up the sails from bolts of Holland duck.

The cotton duck used in the sails of the schooner yacht America was woven at Passaic, N. J., by John Colt, especially for this suit of sails and the way they stood when the America won the cup in English waters in 1851 caused considerable comment in comparison to the bagginess of their cutters' flax sails. In those days and for many years afterwards, it used to be the custom in preparing a small boat for a race, if it was an important one, to hoist and sheet the boat's sail as taut

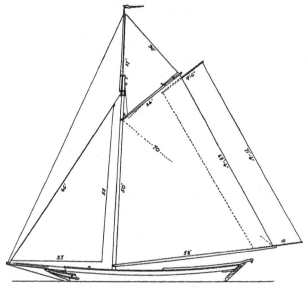

Copy of sail plan of sloop "GEO.H.DAVIS"
Capt. H.Smith dated Sept. 13 ,1855
from the book of sails made by WILSON of Port Jefferson. L.I.
showing a ringtail on the mainsail.

as fiddle strings, then thoroughly wet the sail and allow it to stretch, a sand bag being hung on the end of the boom while the sail was drying in order to stretch the after leech to flatten it.

The general practice among English yachtsmen when

the America arrived there in 1851, was to cut and sew the sails so they would form themselves into a bag to hold the wind, although the advantage of flatness of surface for plying to windward was well understood, and the practice of wetting, or as they termed it, "skeeting" the canvas, was well understood and often employed on board racing boats and ships to flatten their canvas.

We read in histories of the sea fights how the sailors used to hoist up buckets of water and men aloft would throw the water over the sails. The sailors on the

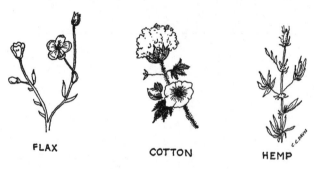

FLAX   COTTON   HEMP

U. S. Frigate Constitution did this when she escaped from the pursuing British fleet on the 19th of June, 1812.

It was a common saying among sailors on English ships as late as 1892, when I went to sea, in referring to the softness of hemp sails compared to the hard cotton ones, "If this were a Yankee ship we'd never get this topsail in this night," for cotton canvas, especially the thick No. oo canvas used on American ships' lower sails, would swell up and become so hard when wet as to make it almost impossible to furl.

Hemp sails you could make a wrinkle in and get ahold of, when muzzling down a topsail in a gale,—but many a time I've seen it when the cotton topsail was so hard the whole crew could not make a wrinkle to get hold of it, and finger nails were broken short off at the

quick. I've gotten up on the bunt of a mainsail or fore-course and jumped on it to stamp down the stiff folds of canvas so the bunt gasket would reach around it.

The soft, pliable, hemp sails used to come and go, so when wet or dry, it used to be said of them, "When they are wet they are double reefed, and when they are dry they are hanging all over the ship."

During war times, when canvas was selling for as high as $1.25 a yard, the New York sailmakers were making sails for deep-water square-riggers out of burlap well soaked with lime, to give them body enough to keep the wind from blowing through them.

To understand the difficulties the sailmaker has to contend with in making a sail, let us see what they are made of, what cotton really is like, and how it is grown.

Cotton is a plant, a species of mallow, that grows abundantly in the warm climates in the form of a shrub from four to six feet high. As the pod or "boll" ripens it bursts and the white cotton fibres are disclosed just as the downy top of a thistle, only cotton is much finer, and on the lower ends of this downy fibre seeds are attached.

Sea Island cotton, grown from seeds imported from the East or West Indies, has a black seed, which distinguishes it from the ordinary cotton with its green seed.

This cotton is picked by hand and separated from its seed by a roller gin or a saw gin. In the former, the raw cotton is fed against a roughened rawhide roller to which the cotton adheres and is drawn under a fixed knife set against this roller, that stops the seeds and a blunt knife operated by machinery tears away the seeds from the down, which is then removed by a wooden roller pressing against the rawhide.

In the saw gin, the cotton is caught up by a set of saws running in a box with narrow slots, which permit the passage of the cotton, but stop the seeds from going through, the cotton is then swept off the sawteeth by brushes revolving faster than the saws. While this method is by far the quicker of the two, the former is not so apt to tear the cotton fibre.

The longer the fibre the more valuable it is, the finest being the Sea Island cotton, as it originally came from the West Indies, where much of it is still obtained, although it is now grown to a great extent in South

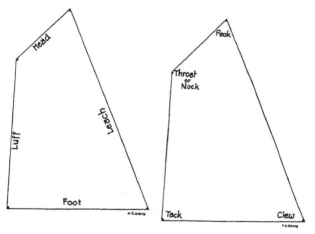

Carolina, Georgia and Florida. Its fibres are from 1⅜ to 2¼ inches in length, glossy, and of a creamy color, with about 300 turns to the inch.

Egyptian cotton ranks next, the fibre being 1⅛ to 1½ inches long, strong, but not quite so fine, showing about 200 turns to the inch.

Brown Egyptian cotton is the most largely grown and

23

used for yachts' sails. Rough Peruvian cotton is 1⅛ to 1⅜ inches long, resembling wool in appearance.

American upland cotton is the ordinary commonly cultivated cotton of the South, about one inch long, fine lustrous, white and strong. India cotton is not as strong, having the shortest fibre.

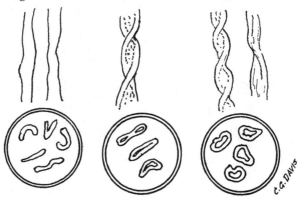

UNRIPE   HALF RIPE   RIPE
COTTON UNDER THE MICROSCOPE

Cotton fibre, under the microscope, shows flattened and twisted spirally, so that when it is spun, the fibres interlock, making a very strong yarn. Short, smooth, untwisted fibres, such as the thistle down, do not adhere but pull apart readily and therefore are of no use for spinning into yarns as cotton is.

These cotton yarns are woven into sail cloth with a smooth, strong surface, the yarns crossing at right angles, are woven just as baskets are made. The yarns running lengthwise of the goods are known as the "warp," the cross strands as the "weft," or filling yarns.

The warp yarns have to be the stronger, as they are the ones that move alternately up and down as the weft strands are laid across between them. To make them strong enough to stand this they are sometimes put through a sizing bath of starch or flour dissolved in boiling water, with some tallow, oil or glycerine mixed in.

If you pick the threads or yarns out of a piece of canvas, you will see the weft strands are almost straight, only slightly dented or corrugated where the other yarns cross them. But the warp yarns show a very decided corrugation like a spring. In weaving a piece of duck the weaver figures that the warp will shorten up 30% due to this corrugation while the weft will shorten only 10%.

The warp strands are twisted up much harder then the weft. In a No. 4 and 6 merchant canvas, for example, the warp strands have a breaking strain of 210 to 240 lb. while the weft strand has a breaking strain of 150 to 170 lb.

Cross-cut sails bring a stretch across the canvas on the weft strands, that is why this type of sail does not last as long as the up-and-down seamed sail.

The flax or linen of which the English sails are made is obtained from the stem of the flax plant. Woven into sail cloth it makes a softer, more springy, cloth that is more inclined to give and bag than the harder cotton cloth which holds its shape better in a hard breeze.

Of late years a great deal of attention has been paid to producing a more perfect sail cloth. The big cup defenders' sails being cut from canvas purposely woven for them.

Yacht designers realize the success or failure of their sail yachts depends as much on the cut and set of the sails as it does on the shape of the boat below water-line.

HISTORICALLY the square sail ranks as the oldest, having been in use for centuries before the lateen sail, the next oldest form of sail, came into use.

Who first used the squaresail is now unknown, but so far as learned investigators can trace back, it was used in Upper Egypt about 6,000 years B. C., while the latter rig has been known since the time of Alexander the Great, about 350 B. C.

The *squaresail* was what the fierce Vikings used on their canoe-shaped craft to relieve the rowers at the heavy sweeps when the wind was fair, as they pursued their venturesome voyages across the stormy North Atlantic.

The *lateen sail,* more suited to light winds, is found around the Mediterranean Sea, Indian Ocean and off the East coast of Africa. Century after century this tall, picturesque rig has survived to the present day.

The *squaresail,* while it has been universally used on ships of any considerable burden for centuries, is an awkward rig for a small boat that has to turn about a great deal—as all small boats do. It requires the services of at least a couple of men to manipulate the tack and sheet, and is an unwieldy thing to handle; so much so, that it was modified first in the form of a *balanced lug-sailing* or a *dipping lug-sail,* which is very similar to a squaresail set fore-and-aft, with the tack set up forward of the mast, very much the same as a squaresail would be trimmed when sailing closehauled.

This in time was changed to a *standing lug-sail,* which by having its tack brought aft to the heel of the mast allowed of tacking without the necessity of shifting the sail every time the boat went about.

While these sails were low down,—simple in that they required only one halyard to raise them— they were a cumbersome sail to stow single-handed; and for this reason a sail was evolved which, by being laced to the

Dipping Lug

mast, could not flop about in the objectionable manner in which a lug-sail was wont to do.

This gave us the *spritsail,* a sail with no halyards at all. Its luff or leading edge being laced to the mast, and the peak set up by a long slender stick called a spreet, now spelled sprit, its upper end in a becket, or loop, of the bolt rope at the top of the sail and the lower

28

end of the sprit set up tight with a becket at the heel of the mast. To reef this sail, the sprit is removed and the whole upper half of the sail folds down. The short spars, the simplicity of the gear and general handiness of this rig made it a great favorite with the fishermen along our coast, particularly in the North, where the winds were fairly strong.

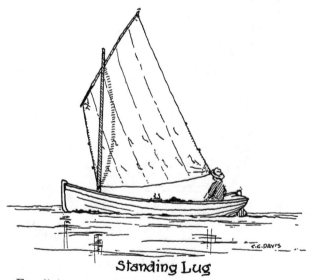

Standing Lug

For lighter breezes in the large sounds and bayous farther South the *leg-o'-mutton sail* was a more popular rig. The narrowness of the sail at its top made it heel a boat but little, and yet by its height it reached up into the higher strata of moving air in calm weather, where a low sail would be becalmed. With its one halyard, no heavy gaff or yard swinging around aloft, there was but little tophamper to heel the boat, and the center of gravity, or center of effort, as yacht designers term that point at which the wind's pressure on a sail is concentrated, being low, particularly suited this sail to the long,

Sprit sail

narrow, canoe-shaped dugouts used by the fishermen in the South.

The leg-o'-mutton sail was also used on the narrow, flat-bottom sharpies peculiar to Connecticut oystermen, who modified it to the extent of cutting off the point at the top just enough to give a *club* about a foot long at the head, which shortened the mast, and still only one halyard was needed. Another modification consisted in cutting off the after corner and spreading the cloth there by the use of a club.

C. G. DAVIS

Leg-o-Mutton.

A club on a sail differs from a boom, in that while the boom goes the full length of the sail, a club is a short spar extending only part way along one edge of a sail, as on a club topsail.

Next to the leg-o'-mutton sail in similarity of shape is the *sliding-gunter*. Here, instead of having a long slender mast, the mast itself is short and the sail is extended up on another spar, a yard, whose lower end is held to the mast by jaws and which stands up straight, parallel to the mast.

Sliding gunther.

This type of sail has proven very popular on the small racing boats of Germany, on the Star class of small boats here in New York waters, and on the small boats of England. The latter are in reality a lug-sail, yet the yard standing vertical, or nearly so, differ only in that it has no jaws holding the lower end of the yard to the mast.

So far as the shape of the sail is concerned it may be said to be the same on all three.

A modification of this gunter rig is the so-called *bat-wing sail,* used largely on racing canoes, and tried out on a few large yachts, the cat-yawl Kuma, of Boston,

C. S. DAVIS

Roslyn rig

for example. On the St. Lawrence River the bat-wing sail was seen as its best along about 1890, when there was keen rivalry between the owners of the skiffs peculiar to the St. Lawrence, and on the Sonder boats of 1913. In this sail a greater area is aimed at by extending the after edge by the use of long wooden battens encased in canvas pockets sewed across the sail radially from the mast.

Cat Yawl KUMA of Boston Mass. with BAT-WING sails

These are the principal types, or families as you might call them, into which sails are divided. The square sail, the oldest of all, had been the most used sail of all.

On ships, large or small, it permitted of an arrangement of spars that could, by the network of braces that held them, hold all the spars secure in any position, and left no swinging spars to slat and bang around as a ship rolled in the swells almost constantly met with at sea.

The sails, by such a rig, were reduced to small squares of cloth easily handled by a few men, and so held that

Type of BAT-WING SAIL used on the St. Lawrence River skiffs.

there was no danger of them slatting themselves to pieces. What wears a suit of sails out the quickest is the slatting they receive as the ship rolls about in the calm weather about the equator. In approaching these latitudes ships have their good sails sent down and an old suit bent on in their place—the newer, stronger sails being rebent when the ship is well North or South of the doldrums, in the strong tradewinds and gales encountered in rounding the Cape or Horn.

In the days when ships carried crews of thirty or

Bat-wing sail.

forty men, when a fast passage meant dollars to the owner, sails were carried that soon went out of use with

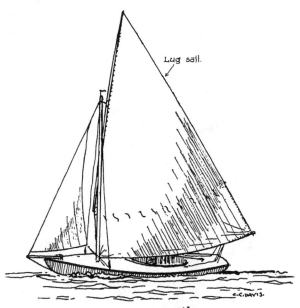

Lug sail.

Lug sail.

the reduction of men in a crew. When, instead of thirty men, a ship put to sea with eight men before the mast, the big single topsails were soon replaced by the double topsails. This added slightly to the weight aloft, but the sail was reduced just one-half in size by the addition of the lower topsail yard. English ships carrying wider topgallant yards also divided these into two sails—upper and lower to'gallant sails. Not generally carrying royals and skysails and moonsails, as the Yankees were wont to do, you could easily distinguish a Lime-juicer as far as you could see one by the stumpy outline of her sails, while a Yankee clipper's sails tapered up into three tall

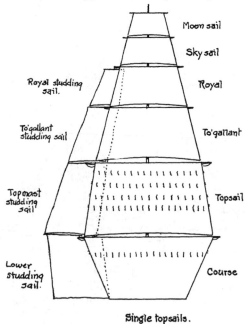

Moon sail

Sky sail

Royal studding sail.

Royal

To'gallant studding sail

To'gallant

Topmast studding sail

Topsail

Lower studding sail.

Course

Single topsails.

Fig. A

pyramids of canvas, the tininess of the little moonsails looking toylike in the distance.

To understand the names of the sails on a square-rigger, look at Figs. A, B and C.

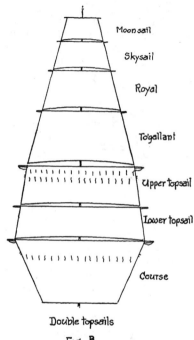

Moon sail

Skysail

Royal

To'gallant

Upper topsail

Lower topsail

Course

Double topsails

Fig. B

In Fig. A we have the old "single topsail" rig with four rows of reefs in the big topsails; in Fig. B we have the "double topsails," with only two rows of reefs in the upper topsail; in Fig. C the "topgallant sails" are doubled.

The names of each sail are the same on all three masts. The lower sail on the foremast being the foresail or fore course, that on the mainmast being the main course, and on the mizzenmast the mizzen, the latter generally called the "cro'jack." Then come the topsails, that on the forward mast being the fore topsail, the next aft the main topsail, and then the mizzen top sail, and

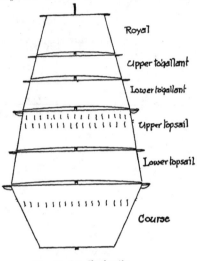

Double to'gallant sails.

Fig. C

so on up on each mast, to the topgallant sails, royals and skysails.

In the fore-and-aft-rigged boats, which more closely concerns us in this day when square-riggers are nearly obsolete, there are a variety of sails which many persons do not know the names of. Sails that have gone out of use entirely are sprung occasionally as a surprise, causing many to guess at the name of the peculiar sail. The racing sloop Nutmeg, sailed so many times to victory

Sloop PHŒNICIA of San Francisco Cal.
with WATER SAIL set under boom.

during 1912 and 1913 by her owner, Mr. A. A. Jones, had a *"ringtail"* that hoisted up along the after edge of her mainsail, the boom and gaff being several feet longer than the mainsail required for this purpose, and considerably increased the sail area for running off the wind.

This sail was but a revival of old times, as the copy of the sail plan of the old sloop Geo. H. Davis, taken from the old books of Sailmaker Wilson, of Port Jefferson, show.

C·G·DAVIS

Sloop NUTMEG of Boston Mass
with RING-TAIL set on main sail.

The ringtail is to the fore-and-aft sail what the *studdingsail* was to the squaresail. Studdingsail booms were spars that extended out beyond the ends of the yards of a ship and on these booms small squaresails

Whaler with a JUMBO foresail.

were hoisted, each taking its name from the sail whose area it increased. (See Fig. A.) On the right-hand side a starboard fore topmast studdingsail would be set, and on the port side the port fore topmast studdingsail, a long name for a small sail. On either side of the top-gallantsails the topgallant studdingsails were set, on either side of the royals the royal studdingsails, etc. The lower ones, those that extended the fore or main course, were

Leg-o·mutton

known as the fore lower studdingsail, or the main lower studdingsail, with the designation port or starboard to show which side was to be set.

Schooners and sloops sometimes set a long narrow strip of canvas under the main boom that hung down to the water, being hauled out to the end of the boom from the deck, known as a *water sail.*

We see none of these sails today; but in the days of pirates and privateers, before steamships were known, every kind of a sail that would increase the ship's speed

Topsail schooner with RAFFEE set.

was resorted to, even to hanging clothes to catch the air that escaped under the roach or foot of one squaresail and the top of the one below it, which were termed *save-alls,* as they saved or made use of all the space the wind could blow upon.

On topsail schooners and whalers, where the crews left on board, when all hands were out in the boats after whales, were small, the work of handling the ship was simplified by having on the foremast, in place of the regular square sail, a *jumbo*, as it was called. This was a triangle sail set point downward and having no sheets or tacks, as a squaresail would, to handle in tacking ship The point of the triangle, being near the deck, was pivoted by a short club or just a clew iron on the foot set up with a single sheet or tackle at the foot of the foremast. Some foresails and mainsails were fitted with this tack clew iron to use when the corners were clewed up, and so converted a squaresail for the time being into a jumbo.

A similar rig, used as a royal or topgallant sail, only set point upward, called a *raffee*, dispensed with a yard and set of braces on short-handed vessels, although some well-manned craft, in the days when sail was crowded on, set small raffees above their royals to make use of every foot of mast-head, for days meant dollars to those ships and quick passages gave big profits.

How Sails are Made

A S the process of making a sail, the actual putting together of the canvas, is interesting, though few yachtsmen understand how it is done and fewer yet have every witnessed the complete process, we will follow a sail through the sail loft.

An order comes in for a cross-cut mainsail. If not too large, it is measured off and chalk lines struck on the sail loft floor; if it is too large, then it is laid off in sections.

Perhaps you have noticed how clean the floors are kept and how the big stove that warms the room is on a platform, suspended by iron rods from the beams overhead, a foot or so off the floor so that the sail cloth can be laid out under it and no room be wasted.

Sometimes the measurements for this sail come in the form of a blue print from a yacht designer, giving the lengths of the spars and an outline of a flat surface the sail is to cover; sometimes the sailmaker has to row out to a yacht and take his own measurements with a tape: in either case the sail in its finished state is far from being a flat plane surface, as the plan would indicate, and it is up to the sailmaker to cut, sew, and rope the canvas into a sail that will give the proper bird's-wing-like surface that has the push and yet will fit those spars. Not exactly fit the spars, either, for sails are of a delicate fabric, not of tin, that will stretch out in time, and the sailmaker must know from experience with each weight of canvas how much it will stretch and make the new sail that much smaller.

He first spreads out and exposes to the weather for

a week or ten days, if he has the time, the canvas that has been tightly rolled up in a bolt ever since it came from the mill.

This equalizes the cloth to the atmospheric conditions.

The foreman meanwhile has marked out the curves or roaches each edge the sail is to have, and on or about the widest part a chalk line is struck across the sail

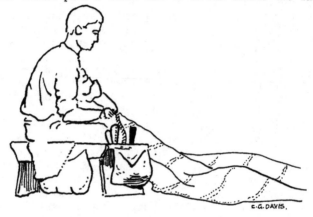

Sailmaker at work.

plan, marked on the floor at right angles to the after leech, the line the seams are to start on.

The breadths of cloth are then rolled out across the sail, the first with its edge along this line, one alongside the other, each being cut outside of the sail's dimensions far enough to allow for the hem or tabling on its edges (see Cross-Cut Sail page 55).

Each succeeding cloth is lapped over the previous

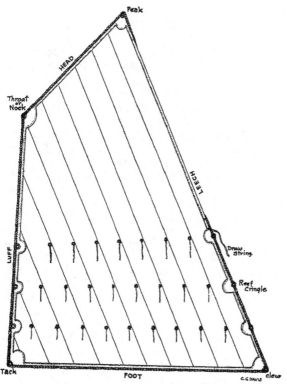

Fig. 1. Sail with Full Width Cloths

one so as to allow a seam for sewing the cloths together. Here is where one of the nice points of sailmaking comes in, in what is called broadseaming the sails. The seams are made narrow at the after edge, ending in an increasing width of seam much wider at the luff or forward edge.

These varying widths are spotted as the cloth lays on the floor, then with a long batten, the seam is marked in a continuous line on the cloth so that the man who sews the cloths together will do so in a fair, true line. In order that the cloths will be sewed together under equal tension without one being tight and the one it is sewed to wrinkled, both are stretched to an equal tension and while so, are marked every foot along their edges.

By watching to see that these marks come together, the operator sewing them on the machine, as they do light canvas, or by hand, if it is heavy canvas, can produce a sail that is perfectly smooth.

After the whole sail is sewed together, it is spread on the floor, its measurements marked according to the draught on the floor and the cloth cut to shape. All the edges, head, foot, luff and leech are given rounds which when bent to straight spars, give the sail its proper draft.

The excess canvas is cut into a strip called the tabling, which is reversed and sewed onto the edge of the sail. This is the general strengthening to the edge of the sail; by being of the same cloth it stretches and shrinks uniformly with the sail. Other strengthening patches are cut and sewed to each corner, where the clew irons are fitted and where the reef cringles come on luff and leech. Small diamond-shape pieces are sewed on at intervals across the sail where the grommets for the reef points are sewed in. Work-boat sails generally have an extra strip of canvas sewed across the sail where the reef points come to strengthen the sail—these are known as reef bands.

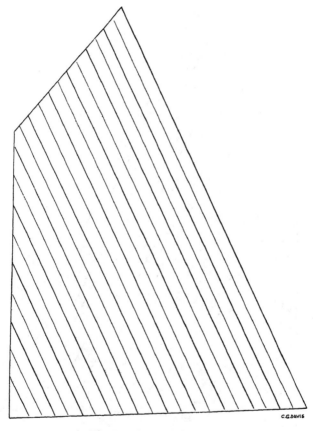

C.G.DAVIS

Fig. 2. Single-Bighted Sail

51

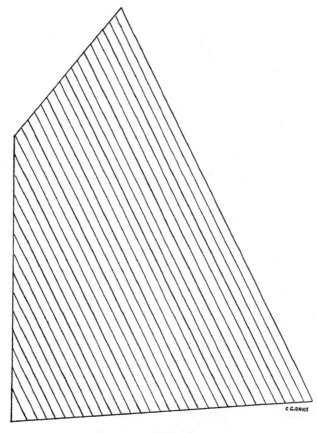

Fig. 3.   Double-Bighted Sail

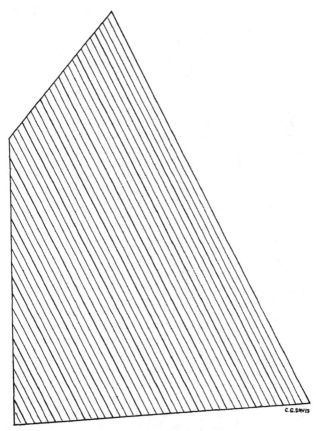

Fig. 4. Triple-Bighted Sail

The main clews are often several thicknesses of cloth and on large sails the outer clew at the end of the main boom, at which point the hardest strain comes on a sail, is sometimes composed of as many as ten thicknesses of cloth in the corner, tapering off in number as they spread out fan-like into the sail.

It takes some sewing machine and some sail needle to sew canvas like this, but they have very powerful sewing machines nowadays, run by electric motors, switched on or off by a pressure of the foot. The needles are about the size of a brad-awl with a score cut far enough up into it so the sail twine lays into this score. Before these needles were invented the twine used to be cut off very often, causing annoyance, loss of time, and a poorer job. But machine-sewed canvas, when properly done, is a far stronger job than hand-sewed, the tension being truer on each stitch, to say nothing of the saving in time. But such machines are expensive.

The twine for the upper thread and that for the lower thread are spun in opposite ways, one being a right-hand twist and one left-handed. Some machines have an automatic feed to the canvas under the needles; in some the needle, itself, shifts back and pulls the canvas along with it, and in some machines, besides having the ordinary feed, which gives the chain stitch, the needle can be set to sew zigzag stitches.

Hand-sewed sails have been extolled for years, but no human being can sew as uniformly as a man of equal skill running a machine. It is true, perhaps, that a hand-sewed sail sewed by an expert is a better job than a machine-sewed sail sewed by an unexperienced person, but that is no comparison—that is an extreme case.

54

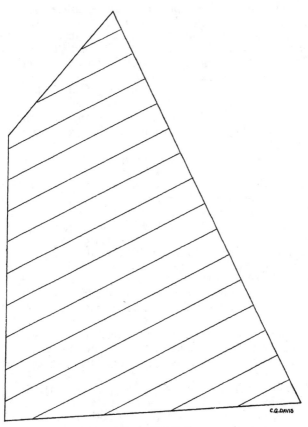

Cross-Cut Sail

55

When the spanker split on the three-masked schooner, J. Percy Bartram, off Hatteras, in 1894, and we spent our watches snake-stitching every seam in that sail before we set it again, I, for one, wished we had a machine aboard that could do the job;— but that's not sailmaking, that is sail repairing.

But while we have been "yamming," what's happened to the sail? It is waiting for its bolt rope.

For fine points in marlinspike seamanship, turning in splices in wire, hemp or manila, the sailmaker cannot be beaten.

Bolt ropes used to be of hemp, but wire for the luff rope has almost entirely superseded it on fine racing boats' sails today, and clew iron, cringles, etc., of iron, brass or composition, are made circular, oval or heart-shaped to suit the occasion.

The way a sailmaker handles rope, unlaying hemp by attaching it to a wheel like a coffee mill and then twisting it up again to soften the lay and make it pliable enough to work, is a revelation to an ordinary yachtsman. They marry strands from a reef cringle into the strands of a wire luff rope or scrape down and rattail a hemp bolt rope for the after leech with apparently the greatest of ease; but practice makes perfect and these are things the ordinary yachtsman is never called upon to do, while the sailmaker does it every day or so. As wire luff ropes are slippery, these ropes are generally hitched with marlin to prevent the canvas sliding or crawling along the stay, as on a jib, where the humps caused by this marlin are easily seen through the canvas covering it. On a mainsail the cloth is sewed right through the wire strands and then covered with canvas besides.

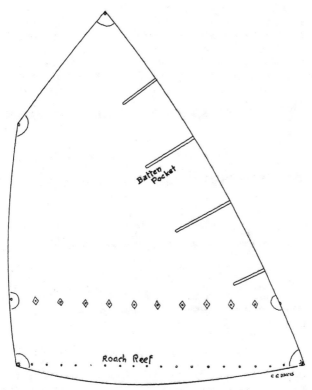

Batten Pocket

Roach Reef

C C DAVIS

Sail with a Roach Reef in the Foot of It

Roping the sail properly is an art. The wire luff rope may be 33 feet, for instance, and the luff of the sail may measure 33 feet 6 inches. The extra 6 inches has to be carefully puckered up along the wire so it does not show; this gives the fullness to the sail where it is needed; were it not done the sail would soon be stretched too flat to be a good driving sail. Along the head and foot ropes, in a similar way, considerable fullness has to be puckered up along the rope near the mast, gradually diminishing towards the leech, until it ends perfectly flat

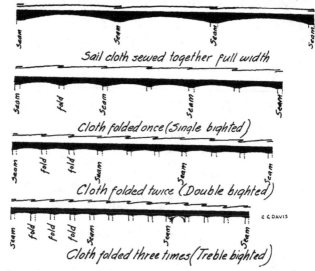

Sail cloth sewed together full width

Cloth folded once (Single bighted)

Cloth folded twice (Double bighted)

Cloth folded three times (Treble bighted)

C G DAVIS

where it is needed so. In putting on the head and foot ropes, they are first pulled with as near the same tension as they will receive when being bent onto the yacht's spars, to stretch them. A colored chalk line is ruled down the edge of each bolt rope and great care taken to stitch the canvas so it lines true along this mark, otherwise the rope might be untwisted or twisted in attaching the canvas.

Along the after leech, inside of the hollow flat hem, a small cotton cord, spliced into the rattail end of the head rope, comes out through a grommet hole just above the reef cringle or down near the clew, giving an adjustable tension to the leech.

Canvas pockets for the wooden battens that help hold up a rounded leech are stitched onto the sail with a grommet hole and short piece of cotton cord called a "nettle," to tie the end of the batten in so it cannot work out. Such excessive roaches have been carried on sails in recent years in attempts to cheat the rules, which measure the mainsail area in a straight line from peak cringle to clew cringle, that a rule has been passed limiting the length of the battens to a certain percentage of the boom's length—110% for the upper and lower battens plus one foot, and 112% for the two intermediate battens plus one foot.

If one has never done any marlinspike seamanship they cannot fully appreciate the niceties of the way some of the cringles are turned into the clews of some sails, even being backed up by lashings or seizings through extra grommet holes worked back farther into the cloth, or with two tail-like sennet braids laid on the clew patches and sewed to them to help take up the heavy pull the clew cringle gets.

For shipment, sails are rolled up in heavy paper and old canvas, sewed up so as to be well protected from dirt in transit; and as a precaution against abusing the new sail in bending it, tags are sometimes attached to head and foot clews, giving the exact length the sail should be bent to at first. Even then I have seen men, who thought they knew more about the sail than the man who made it, put a tackle on and stretch a new sail all out of shape. The trouble is, the head and foot stretch too quickly. To handle a new sail properly is to keep the head and foot only just tight enough so it will not wrinkle, and give the middle of the sail a chance to stretch out evenly with the edges.

The old style of making sails was to sew the strips of canvas so the seams ran up and down from gaff to boom, parallel to the after leech of the sail. All working-boat sails are made in this way, as they last longer than the new style of cross-cut sails. (Figs. 1, 2, 3, 4)

Canvas comes in "bolts," as rolls are called, and vary in width from 14 inches to 24 inches or more. As the edges of these breadths were sewed together or "seamed," the double thickness in the lap of this seam naturally was stronger and stretched less than the single thickness of the cloth. This produced a series of ridges and hollows in the very light cloth used for yacht's sails and made a very poor surface for the wind to sweep across, as in Fig. 1.

To prevent this sagging between seams the sails were "single-bighted," as in Fig. 2, the cloth being folded and sewed so it made apparently another seam, but it was really only a fold, or as sailors call a fold, a "bight." A bight of a rope is when it lays in a loop, and so this kind of a sail is termed a single-bighted sail. In a single-bighted sail the distance between bights was cut in half and consequently the sag in the cloth was very much reduced.

While this added slightly to the weight of a sail, the advantage in the better setting of the canvas, the smoother surface it gave, more than compensated for the weight. So much so that another bight was tried with even better results, giving what was called a "double-bighted" sail, as shown in Fig. 3.

For years this was the favorite style of sail in racing boats, and a man was very proud of the fact that his boat had a "double-bighted" sail, and in advertising her for sale this fact was generally mentioned. Treble-bighted sails have been made but not often.

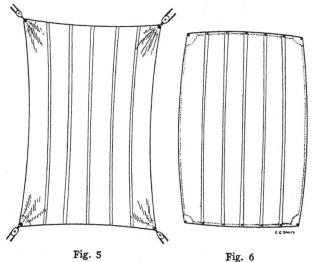

Fig. 5   Fig. 6

The cross-cut sail came into vogue about the same time the so-called shovel-nosed bow did—neither being a new idea, but had not before been popular.

In these sails the seams, instead of running parallel

61

with the leech, were run at right angles to it, nearly horizontally across the sail. The pull here being across the seams, no bights were needed and the canvas was used its full width.

The famous sloop yacht Maria, built at Hoboken, N. J., in 1844, from designs by A. L. Stevens, had a set of cross-cut sails, but these were at that time far too expensive for the ordinary yachtsman. Today the cross-

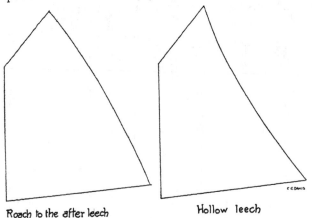

Roach to the after leech   Hollow leech

cut sail is used extensively as a racing sail and is of finely woven texture, as fine as any dress goods.

Canvas, if pulled either lengthwise of the goods or across the goods, is firm and comparatively unyielding; but when pulled diagonally, "on the bias," or obliquely across the texture of the goods, all cloths stretch considerably. As three edges of a mainsail are so cut, some provision has to be made to allow for this stretch. Even if it were a perfectly square sail, some allowance must be made for the constant strain that is to come on the corners, which would soon pull a sail out, as shown in Fig. 5.

This the sailmaker provides for and also gives some curve or fullness to the sail by what is termed "broadseaming." The edges of the sail are shortened by gradually widening the seam or lap of the cloths where they are sewed together, from the middle toward the edges, as shown in Fig. 6.

Even when so seamed a double-bighted sail would, if not carefully handled and hauled out too hard on peak and clew, be changed in shape, forming a hollow leech. The roping on the edge of the sail also takes care of some of this stretch, the sail being slightly puckered up or "pulled" along the rope so that when the rope stretches, as it is bound to do to a certain extent, the cloth will not be stretched any but just come out smooth and flat.

If this broadseaming were not done, and if the sail were cut straight between corners, where would the sail get the slack necessary to give that curved surface which we call its draft? Such a cut sail would, when the wind pressed on it, pull up into a shape like Fig. 7, and if the cloth were not there to allow of this, the spars would bend that way.

It is apparent that the cloth from A to B in Fig. 8 must be longer to allow it to curve out as in Fig. 9 as a sail must when the wind blows upon it, and therefore the cloths must be cut with a curve or "roach," as it is technically called more or less according to the fullness or flatness of the sail desired, as in Fig. 10. Cloths of this length when the middle of the sail bellies out will give straight edges along the gaff and boom.

In the same way the curved dotted line C-D, across the sail in Fig. 11 will, when straightened out, come out to the points E-E, showing that fullness must be properly allowed for in some way, and that sailmaking is a far more scientific business than awning making, as many a man who has tried to get a cheap sail has found out.

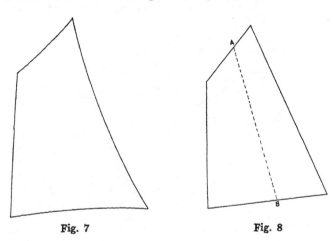

Fig. 7   Fig. 8

Different sailmakers have different theories on just how much of this curve, or roach, there should be and on which edge of the sail it should be allowed, some allowing a great deal more on the foot than others.

Realizing that considerable fullness, or draft, is an advantage in light airs and that flatter sails are better in a hard blow, in order to combine the two in one sail some sails are cut with excessive fullness along the boom and then fitted with a row of reefing eyelets, in order that this bagginess may be laced or tied up with reef points to flatten the sail in a breeze. This is known among yachtsmen as a "roach reef," the curve to the edge of the sail being known as the roach, and was first used by that veteran yacht designer, Mr. A. Cary Smith, on the sloop yacht Regina.

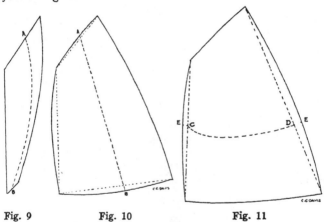

Fig. 9   Fig. 10   Fig. 11

This term, "roach," is incorrect. A roach properly is a concave curve along the foot –cut with a sweep is really correct; but as this is one of those errors made permissible by universal practice, we shall continue to call the full sail cut with a sweep—a roached sail.

In light weather or heavy weather the closely woven cotton sails hold all of the wind, but the old-time flax sail cloth was like a sieve and the air escaped through it to such an extent wetting the canvas was a common practice on racing yachts. Small racers carried a long light stick with a cow-horn lashed on its end for dipping up and sprinkling the water on the sails. This instrument was known as a "skeet" and in the old English yacht club rules, to prevent its being used as a paddle, "skeeting" to windward only was allowed.

Center of Effort, Area and
Shape of Mainsails

IN one respect a man has a free hand at deciding upon what shaped sail he wants for his boat, but in another there are a few natural laws, their principles as simple as that which operates a weather vane and yet as exacting as all nature's laws are—this is the law of balance, which must be observed.

He may make his rig low and broad or high and narrow, but the center of effort, that mysterious "center" that confuses so many amateurs, must be in its proper relation to the center of lateral resistance of the hull.

If you were to try to push a heavy beam lying on a perfectly smooth floor, you would not be surprised if you were to push the beam near one end if that end swung around away from you; you would expect it. You would try to push as near the middle as possible so it would not turn. Now the center of effort is the same as that place where you pushed on the log and the center of lateral resistance is just what its name says it is, the center where it evenly resists being pushed sideways.

The center of lateral resistance of a boat is that point where, if a line were made fast, she would tow evenly sideways through the water. A knowledge of its fore-and-aft position so determined is sufficient to be able to design a sail plan that will balance it. The center of the sails must be not quite directly over it, but just a few inches ahead of it, more or less, as the boat be bluff-bowed or fine. As a bluff-bowed boat heels over and moves ahead, she piles the water up under the lee bow and this resistance requires a certain amount of side push from the forward sails to balance it.

If the center of such a boat's sails were directly over the center of lateral resistance figured as she stands upright, she would luff so hard you could not keep her out of the wind.

The finding of the center of effort of a sail plan is a simple example in triangles. The center of effort or center of gravity, for both mean the same thing, of a jib, for instance as in Fig. 12, is found by measuring up from the middle of the foot of the jib one-third the distance to the head, there is its center of effort.

Graphically, it may be found with no calculations whatever. Cut the shape of the sail out of cardboard. Hang it up by a pin in one corner. Drop a plumb line from this pin and mark where it crosses the sail. Then hang it up by another corner and where the plumb line crosses the first one is the center of gravity. This method may be used on any shape of sail—mainsail, jib topsail, etc.

Another way is to draw a line from the middle of the foot of the jib to the head as in Fig. 12, and another line from half-way up the luff or hoist of the jib to the clew. Where these two lines cross is the center of effort, the same spot as found in Fig. 12, and practically the same as the plumb-bob method.

Its area in square feet is found by multiplying the length of the luff in feet by one-half the distance to C, in Fig. 13, measured across at *right angles* to the luff.

The mainsail may be calculated as if it were two triangles, if one is not versed in figures.

Divide the mainsail into two triangles, Fig. 14, by

The Tall Sail on Presto

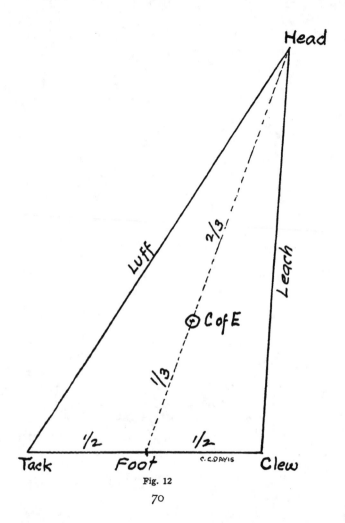

Fig. 12

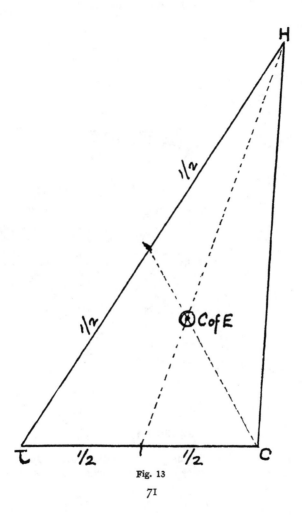

Fig. 13

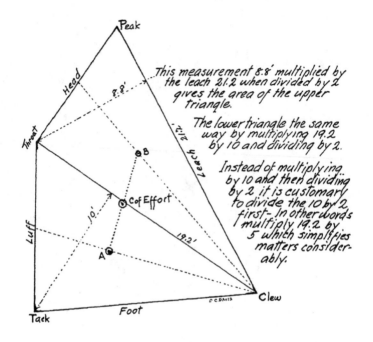

Peak

Head

8.8'

Throat

Luff

Leach 21½'

B

C of Effort

10'

A

19.2'

Tack

Foot

Clew

This measurement 8.8' multiplied by the leach 21.2 when divided by 2 gives the area of the upper triangle.

The lower triangle the same way by multiplying 19.2 by 10 and dividing by 2.

Instead of multiplying by 10 and then dividing by 2 it is customary to divide the 10 by 2 first- In other words multiply 19.2 by 5 which simplifies matters considerably.

C.C.DAVIS

Fig. 14

drawing a line from the throat to the clew. Find the center of each of these triangles the same as you did

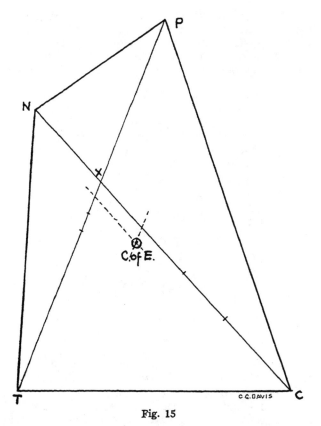

Fig. 15

for the jib. This gives you two centers, A in the lower
triangle, B in the upper.

To find the common center, as it is called, draw a line connecting these two. Somewhere on this line proportional to their areas is this common center. If both were of the same area, the center would be midway. To calculate it you must know the area of each triangle.

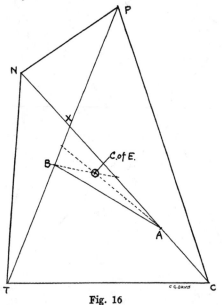

Fig. 16

There are two dimensions in figuring areas of triangles, length and breadth, but they must be measured at right angles to each other. The area of a triangle is just one-half of the product obtained by multiplying the length of the longest side of the triangle by the greatest breadth measured at right angles to it. The three illustrations given show how the areas of the angles equal one-half of the area of length and breadth, no matter what the shape may be or where the greatest breadth is measured. The lower triangle of our sail equals 96 square feet, the upper one 93.3 Calculating from the center of the lower triangle set down the fiigure 96 and multiply it by zero ; under it write the upper triangle and multiply it by the distance between the centers A and B, in this case 7 feet. The product, 653.1, divided by the sum of both triangles, 189.3, gives the distance the center of effort of the whole sail is above A, measured along the dotted line to B.

There is a graphic way of laying out the center of effort that is more difficult to describe than to do. Draw two lines from corner to corner, as shown in Fig. 15. Measure off the distance N-X, and set it off on the line up from C, and the same with the distance P-X, setting it off from T. Divide the distances from these points to X into three equal parts and through the inner third mark (the nearest to X), draw lines parallel to the two diagonal lines first drawn and where they cross you have the center of effort.

Another way of finding this center of effort is to draw the two diagonal lines as in Fig. 15. Set off the distance from N to X, up along the line from C. (clew). And from T (tack), measure up the distance P (peak) to X. Draw a line A B, as in Fig. 16, and you have a triangle in the middle of the sail. The center of this is found by drawing a line from halfway between X and B to A and halfway between A and X to B. Where they cross is the center of effort of the sail.

To find the center of effort of a mainsail and jib

combined, or with clubtopsail and jib, as in Fig. 17, the operation is merely a repetition of the calculation you have made for finding the center of the mainsail by dividing it into two triangles. In this all the centers are measured from a vertical line drawn up through the center of the mainsail; this is done to reduce the calculations to small figures. The result would be the

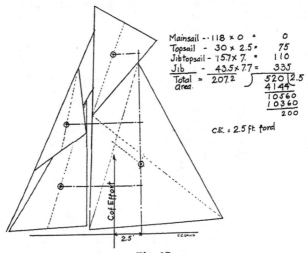

Mainsail -- 118 × 0 =   0
Topsail - 30 × 2.5 =   75
Jibtopsail - 15.7 × 7. =   110
Jib   - 43.5 × 7.7 =   335
Total = 207.2) 520 2.5
area.   4144
                      ──────
                      10560
                      10360
                      ──────
                        200

C.E. = 2.5 ft. ford

Fig. 17

same if, as in Fig. 18, all the centers were measured from a perpendicular line ahead of the boat. In the same manner, if desired, the height of this center can be calculated by measuring from the water-line up to each center, as in Fig. 19, multiplying by the areas of each sail and dividing the results.

76

For a schooner or yawl sail plan, the center of effort is found the same way. Yacht designers generally figure the distance the center of each sail is forward or aft of the center of lateral resistance. It seems more com-

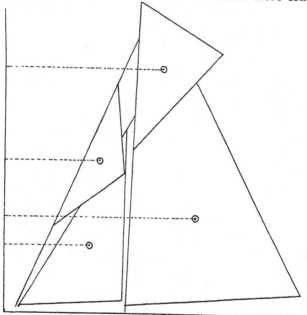

Fig. 18

plicated to the novice to do it this way, but when you get used to it you will find it is as simple as the other methods.

Here (see Fig. 20), we have the center of the mainsail aft of the vertical line drawn up through the center of lateral resistance, while the jib and staysail are forward. In calculating these the product of the mainsail area multiplied by its moment (as the distance from the line to the center of effort is called), being aft, is subtracted from the sum of the products of the jib and staysail multiplied by their moments. This difference is then divided by the total sail area, as in Fig. 17, and the quotient is the distance the center of effort of the whole sail plan is forward or aft of the vertical line, according to whether the products of the headsails or that of the mainsail be the greater. The importance of understanding this question of balance between the centers is considerable. You realize what is taking place when a boat begins to steer hard and know the remedy.

Take as an example a jib and mainsail sloop: She hangs beautifully at first and steers easily. After a month or so the owner finds that his boat is carrying a hard helm, and I have seen several men go to the sail loft and have their boat's mainsails recut to clear their heads; the booms had come down as the canvas stretched, they said. As a matter of fact, trimming down hard of the mainsheet and hammering the boat through heavy weather had stretched the headstay and bobstay, letting the masthead aft and this in turn lowered the boom-end considerably, as you can see by a glance at Fig. 21. It also moved the center of effort far enough aft to cause a hard helm. All that was needed was to set up on the headstay and pull the mast forward where it was intended to be.

The owners of the Boston raceabouts, realizing the nicety of balance that could be obtained by a slight shift

78

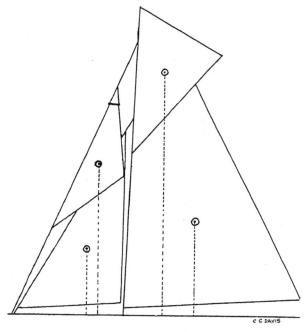

Fig. 19

of the mast, used to fit their mast in a slot in the deck
so it could be shifted forward or aft, until a perfect
balance was struck. Their chain plates to receive the
shrouds consisted of an angle-iron at the deck edge,

79

with a row of holes to bolt the turnbuckles to, permitting quite a range of adjustment to the shrouds.

For light airs the mainboom gooseneck was shoved up the mast a couple of feet, and in heavy weather it was

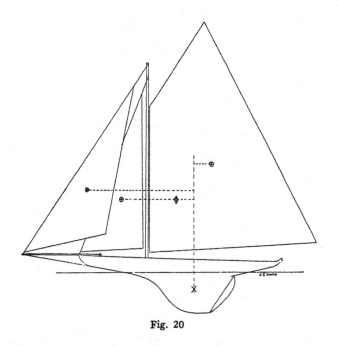

Fig. 20

dropped down—this was done because the sail area was limited to a certain number of square feet.

Where the areas are thus limited, the problem of

selecting the best proportioned sail for the local wind conditions becomes important and past experience has shown that the high narrow rig with its long cutting edge, just as in the aeroplane and racing propeller blade,

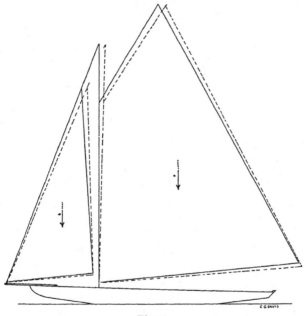

Fig. 21

is the most efficient. The lifting or propeller reaction of the air upon a surface depends upon the amount of air displaced or acted upon by it in a unit of time. In Fig. 22 the figures in the planes, *A, B* and *C,* represent their respective lifting values, all having the same number of square feet. By this we see that *B* with its long cutting edge has four times the lifting value of *C*.

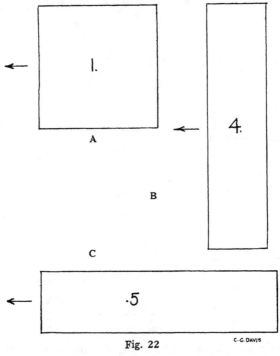

Fig. 22

C.G. DAVIS

When we come to apply this principle to sails, we find there are other limiting features to be considered. The flexibility of the sail which forms the plane acted upon by the wind, requires a certain breadth along the boom to be able to hold the gaff in where it belongs.

One of the narrowest, loftiest rigs I can remember

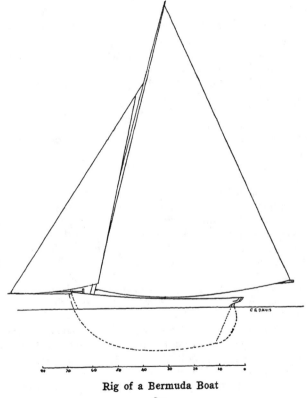

Rig of a Bermuda Boat

83

was on the sandbag catboats Presto, Tattler and Phyllis —to bring their gaffs in so the sail aloft was pulling, the foot was swigged down to the end of a wide horse, so the foot of the sail was flat as a sheet of tin.

The old Connecticut sharpie rig was a high, narrow one of two sails and so was the famous Block Island rig.

Bermuda boats have a tall leg-o'-mutton rig hove flat with a sprit-like boom set taut with a tackle part way up the sail, similar to the sharpie.

The Sonder boats carried rigs much shorter on the foot than the length of the boat, and nearly all the fast boats, we find, have this same characteristic, so when it is scientifically backed up by flying machine demonstrations, there is little room to doubt the efficiency of the narrow rig.

In Europe, today the racing rig on the small boat has developed in an excessively tall, narrow leg-o'-mutton sail, with a polemast trussed with spreaders to prevent its bending and made automatic in its adjustment of the sails by a light wide headstay. By hauling on this and keeping the mast straight, the bag in the luff is retained, or by slacking this headstay, the masthead is allowed to bend aft and the sail flattens itself out. The shape of the sail has undergone a great many changes—all an evolution from the squaresail—but for yacht work, for handiness and all-around weatherliness, the present shaped mainsail is the best.

As the model of the boat has changed from time to time, the shape of the sail has been changed also. To illustrate this point, look at the shape of the sails used on the yachts of 1850, with their short gaffs. Boats in their days did not have lead keels; they carried inside ballast and did not have the stability a heavy lead keel gave to carry a square-headed sail.

The small sandbaggers of a few years later, however, had a radically different sail—a very square-headed sail. They, by piling many sandbags on the weather deck edge, had excessive stability. Today, we have a modification of the two. Our racers of today carry a lead bulb keel, hung low under the hull, and the tendency year by year has been to a higher, narrower rig. The early fin keelers, such as the Larchmont 21-footers, Houri, Celia, Vaquero and Adelaide, had a low rig, long on the foot to keep the center of pressure low down, but this rig has gradually developed into a narrow, high one.

Mr. C. W. Foster, of Boston, an enthusiastic owner of Sonder boats, eliminated all doubt as to which was the best sail for a Sonder boat by having a turntable built upon his lawn and on this testing out various shaped sails until he evolved one that gave more push than any of the others, and judging from his success, his efforts in this were rewarded. Sails have been used before on turntables, but for a far different purpose. In the days when steam plants were a luxury, Peter Sherwood ran a sawmill at New Rochelle, N. Y., which received its power from a large turntable built on the roof of a two-story shop located in the rear of what used to be the old Bedeau property on Center Avenue, near the Trinity Schoolhouse.

A ring of small sails, luffing, pulling and jibing, was a common sight to the school children, and it was one of these sails whose use was abandoned when a steam plant was installed, that was the first sail Captain Thomas R. Webber, builder of many sailboats, had for his first real sailboat.

85

Proper Shape and Trimming for Jibs

THE proper shape, make and handling of the head-sails comes next in importance to the mainsail. It must not only be a good setting sail in itself, but it must do so without backwinding and so impairing the utility of the mainsail. The two must work in harmony.

In America, the single jib with its lower section re-

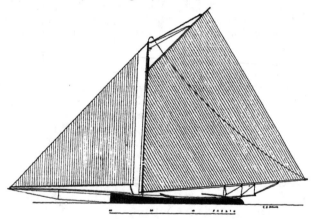

Sail Plan of Sandbag Sloop Dare Devil

movable and called the bonnet, was in favor for a great many years. It was not until about 1888 the craze for the cutter rig spread among yachtsmen in this country and the double headsail, consisting of a staysail hoisting on a stay that set up to the gammon iron at the stem head, and a jib at the end of the bowsprit came into use to any extent. Yachts up to that time had followed the packet sloop and fishing smack rig, using one big jib.

The advantages of the double head rig as used on cutters, were the fact that the headsails, being in two pieces, it was much easier to reduce the area by taking in one of them; that the jib being hooked to an iron ring, or traveler as it was called, encircling the bowsprit could be hauled out without having a man go out on the bowsprit, and in taking in the jib, its tack could be hauled in to the stem head and the jib unhooked without a man leaving the deck. An even more important feature for seagoing work was the fact that the staysail was set on a forestay, that, should the bowsprit be carried away, would hold the mast secure and the whole rig would not go by the board, overboard.

But when the owners of sloops imitated this rig they only copied half of it. The best features they omitted; they shackled their jibs to the end of the bowsprit, and to stow that sail one had to lay out on the bowsprit and generally got soaked in doing so.

Many sloops with a small single jib, when altered to a double head rig, had two narrow slats of canvas too long and narrow to be of any use as driving sails. Regardless of this fact many sloops were so altered. The charm of being able to say a man owned a cutter proved too much for those who yachted for style without understanding the fitness of the rig as applied to their particular boat.

Sandbaggars carried the single jib to the extreme in the 70's. Boats like the famous Dare Devil, 28 feet long, had a sail plan 72 feet on the base from the end of her 40-foot mainboom to the end of her bowsprit. The jib was 30 feet on the foot and the same on the leech; her mainsail hoisting 28 feet. Most of these boats had the foot of the jib laced to a long, thin jibboom, with double jib sheets rove through sister blocks, or where lightness was desired, *lignum vitae* bull's eyes were used. The tack of the jib was shackled to an eye-bolt on top of the bowsprit eye-band or wythe. All the racers had jibs with hemp ropes set flying. The boat's mast was stepped with a decided rake aft and held, when the jib was lowered, by a light wire stay. The jib when set was hoisted hard enough to slacken this stay, but even then the luff of the jib was inclined to sag off a little. Boats in those days carried no backstays; when the mainsheet was flattened down it was supposed to tighten the luff of the jib.

Marine hardware was at that time very crude. Blacksmiths forged eye-bands or wythes as they were called, and goosenecks, but you could not go to a store and buy them. Some had a long-necked eye-bolt on top of the bowsprit to take the tack of the jib and around the shank of this eye-bolt a swiveled clevis was fitted, into which an eye-bolt in the end of the jibboom toggled.

Larger sloops had these jibbooms swiveled to a gooseneck that slid back and forth on an iron horse or traveler on top of the bowsprit. This slide allowed the jib to come down all the way when lowered; this the jib would not do otherwise, the jib being set on hanks hooked to the jibstay, as the distance A to B will not reach to C, the end of the bowsprit by the distance C to D, Fig. 23. The slide must be the length, C to D, to let the point B forward that much. The sandbagger's jibs being set flying, came down with no trouble except to muzzle them down and prevent their getting overboard and wet.

There was in those days, as there is yet, considerable argument as to the advantages or disadvantages of a jib boom or a loose footed jib. A jib is, just as the lug sail or the lateen sail on an Arab dhow, a lifting sail; and many claim that the boom on the foot of a jib

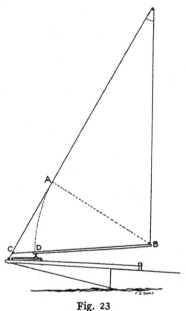

Fig. 23

destroys this lifting effect by preventing the wind's free flow out of the foot of the sail. That was why the English cutters always had "loose footed" mainsails.

A far more vital point however was the proper curve

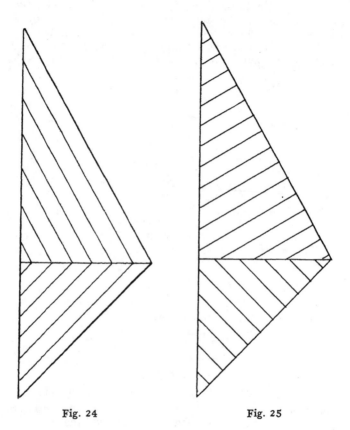

Fig. 24   Fig. 25

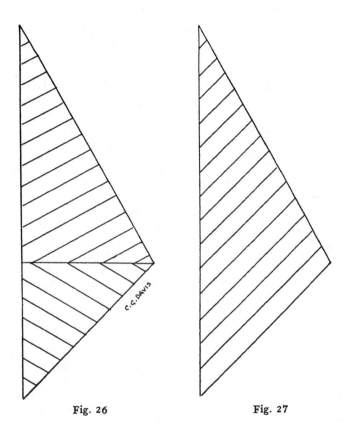

Fig. 26   Fig. 27

or draft in the sail. The same parabolic curve should be in the jib as in the mainsail. This, in the vertical seamed jib, as in the mainsail, was obtained by cutting the cloth with a full roach on the luff, by broadseaming and by being roped full along the luff rope. You can sew a sail to a rope in such a way that the sail is tightly stretched along the rope, or "full it" by gathering the sail cloth up so it is slack, though of course it doesn't show wrinkles along the rope.

Where a jib is cut with cloths running up and down parallel to the after leech, the diagonal cut across the goods along the stay or luff, being on the bias, is very easily stretched, and here is where in roping a jib, the cloth must be sewed slack or "fulled."

The greatest strain on such a jib comes across the weakest edge of the cloth, the hoist, and yet if this be reversed and the gores put along the leech and foot, they go out of shape and a hard spot from clew to luff cuts the sail into two bags. The leech and foot are the edges that must be a perfect flattened curve, as the proper escape for the wind is all important, and to obtain this flattened curve, various compromises have been tried, as shown in Figs. 24, 25, 26 and 27.

Wire luff ropes have almost entirely superseded the hemp ones in modern yacht sails, as that has far less stretch, and the continual strain on a luff rope of a jib is quite severe. The proper making of a jib is important, but to set it properly is of equal importance and a point not understood as is should be. The object of a jib is not to be a bag to catch wind, but a fair curve along the luff with a perfectly flat smooth leech, so after the wind has pushed the sail all it could, the wind has a free chance to escape. Any part of the after edge of the jib that offers resistance to this free flow of the wind is worse than useless; it is a hindrance.

In many cases a perfectly good jib is not sheeted so it gives the greatest amount of forward pull on account of the angle the jib sheets are fitted, most of them being too close in toward the mast. In a fore-and-aft direction, the jib sheets should put just a trifle more strain on the foot of the jib, pulling it flat aft, than it does on the after leech. As to how wide the sheets should lead, they should be so that the jib's luff begins to flutter just before the luff of the mainsail, when both sails are flattened down for windward work.

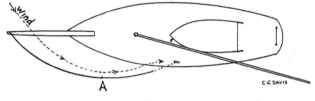

Fig. 28

Sheets too far aft are bad; they pull the after leech of the sail so tight the whole after edge forms a back sail; sheets too far forward free this leech and lose some of the jib's power by the flowing up and fluttering of loose cloths in the leech.

The after leech of the jib should approximate the same curve as the mainsail's surface as you look at a boat from the lee quarters.

Too wide a lead on the jib sheet is better than one too narrow, for the latter pulls the after edge of the jib

93

in so it forms a curve which pushes the boat astern, while the curve in the luff is attempting to push her ahead. To stop a boat, to "heave to" as it is called, the jib is pulled in amidships or to windward and you certainly are not trying to stop your boat, so look carefully to see that the jib sheets lead properly, for you not only lose power in the jib, but by interfering or backwinding hurt the mainsail as well.

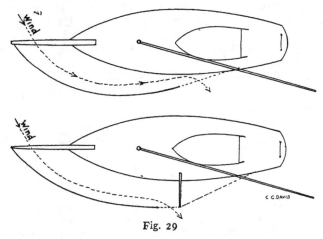

C. C. DAVIS

Fig. 29

One would think when a man has a racing sloop where the trim of jib and mainsail are as perfect as can be made by properly adjusted trim of the sheets, that when he came to set a balloon jib he would know how to set and sheet it, but there are many who don't. Hoisting the sail up tight does not make it pull. It is then the adjusting of them to the proper angle in relation to

94

the strength and direction of the wind that makes the boat go faster or slower.

Here again as in the jib, the greatest evil is in pulling the after edge of the jib in so it makes a back sail. These very light cloths are more inclined to bag than the heavier working sails, and greater care is needed in handling them. It is not so much the size of the balloon sail as it is the number of square feet in that sail that are pulling to advantage, especially on a reach.

You often see a sloop with the wind abeam in a hard blow where half of the balloon jib is a back sail, that much of it from the extreme outer point of the bag in the middle of the sail is pulled in again towards the center of the boat so the wind has to come in around its edge.

If the canvas in such a sail could be cut off at *A, Fig.* 28, at which point the wind has exerted all the forward push possible, the resistance of all that wind against the rest of the sail would be avoided and the boat would go just so much faster.

Many boats on a hard reach need this bag in their headsails to help steer them; but an evil, as I call defects in a boat's design, should not be remedied by adding another evil in the sails to balance it. If you want a racer correct the first evil by restepping the mast.

Where the hull, as many are, is too narrow to properly sheet the ballooner, an outrigger to spread the width of the balloon jib-sheet lead, will result in an increase in speed, Fig. 29.

This was done in the 34-raters class of 1895. On Dragoon an oak board could be slipped under cleats on deck and the balloon jib sheet rove through bull's-eyes either 4 feet or 6 feet out from the lee rail. In classes where outriggers are, as is sometimes the case, prohibited, a man sitting to leeward can hold this sheet out with one foot and so increase the pulling power of the balloon jib.

It looks as if a boat were traveling fast and artists delight in drawing the luff of the balloon jib arched away off to leeward, but every foot the stay sags off means a tremendous loss of power. Remember it's the curve in the

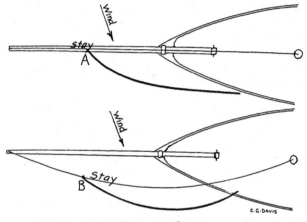

Figs. 30 and 31

luff that drives the boat ahead. So set the weather backstays and runners up hard and try to hold the luff of the jib in a straight line. When this is done, the jib makes a good propelling curve, as in Fig. 30; but if the stay slacks off to leeward the luff, instead of holding this curve, sags off from *A*, where the stay should be, to *B* in Fig. 31 so that the sail is nothing but a saucer-shaped surface that pushes back as much as it does forward and the sail merely drags the boat's head off to leeward.

This often occurs on a reach with a hard wind abeam. Many yachtsmen make the mistake of carrying too much sail in a hard beam wind. Burying the lee rail so everything is dragging through the water to leeward, tearing it into foam, does not necessarily mean the boat is going the fastest she is capable of.

Action of the Wind

FIN keel boats with their round cigar-shaped hulls and thin metal fins travel just as fast laid over on their beam's end as upright, so long as they are trimmed so the fin cuts straight through the water, but, if by her crew sitting too far aft, the fin is presented the least bit sideways, the resistance is immediately noticeable.

The little fin keel Star Class boats noticed this, and to keep their fins edge on the crews have to sit well forward so much so that the tiller was lengthened on some to allow the helmsman to get his weight forward.

On knockabout type of boats, and by them we mean, boats built with wooden fins to support the lead keels, the mistake is often made of making the boat too full in the garboards, or the top of the wooden fin keel too thick.

When such a model heels over, the lower diagonal lines are so full aft the water comes boiling out from under the boat in a roll of white foam off the weather quarter. Her speed is limited to the speed with which the water can flow under this part of the boat. As soon as she tries to go faster she attempts to drag a vacuum in the water and this creates a resistance that is considerable. The roll of foam under the bow does not take anywhere near the power to make it that this dragging wave does aft.

Different boats require different treatment to get the best speed out of them due to some peculiarity of the hull. In 1895, when the 15-foot water-line class of boats called half-raters (because they rated ½ under the English system of racing measurement) were in their prime, there were two boats built by Herreshoff, one called the Gnome, the other Olita. One day in a race off New Rochelle these two boats started last of a class of about eight boats.

Soon after the start, the wind hauled fair, a man on the Olita went forward to bend on her big balloon jib, and we from a distance saw Olita pick up and go much faster. She passed several boats and at the rate she was

Australian Twenty-One-Footer

sailing would soon have been the leader; with her peculiar square stern and long overhanging bow, the man's weight had put this bow down and lifted the stern so her sailing lines were very much easier. But neither of her crew seemed to notice the improvement. The man went aft again and Olita stopped as if a brake had been applied.

99

But there was another boat built later on the same principle; rule cheaters, these boats were called, because while they measured short on the water-line at anchor, when they heeled they lengthened their side in the water considerably. That boat was the 30-foot racing catboat Volsung and her crew utilized every advantage of the

Connecticut Sharpie

hull. It was a common sight to see Volsung driving to windward in a heavy sea with two men encased in oil-skins lying flat and hanging onto her deck forward of the mast.

There is another advantage in shifting the crew's

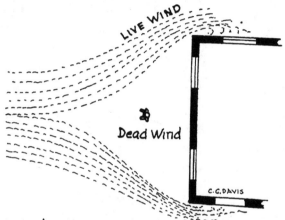

If the wind is blowing squarely against the wall of a building you will find a wedge shaped space of dead wind.

Fig. 32

weight that can be employed on small boats where the weight of the crew amounts to something compared to the weight of the hull, and that I picked up one day, years ago, when we were beating down the Hudson River in our catboat Rambler from Yonkers to 152d Street. Off

Spuyten Duyvil we met the cat Roma. Tack after tack, our wide sandbagger, sailed at that time with only six sandbags and a small sail, kept nose and nose with Roma with her fixed iron ballast stowed along under her floor. Off Fort Washington Point the ebb tide kicked up a sea and from here, every time the two boats jumped, Roma forged ahead a foot or so. I soon figured out what was doing it and had Bill, my brother, put three sandbags

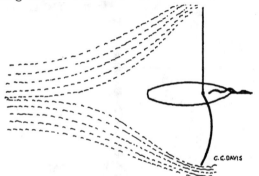

If mainsail and spinnaker are both squared off the live wind goes out around them and dead wind only presses on the sails,-

Fig. 33

up near the mast and three on the after deck: the result was noticeable. Rambler was slower to jump and slower in her swing and from then on foot by foot, every wave, we came up on and passed the Roma. Do you suppose such lessons were forgotten? Try such stunts next Summer but don't try any you can't give a reason for.

Accidents do sometimes supply knowledge, as my old friend A. Cary Smith once experienced; when in a light wind, the outhaul to the mainsail carried away, the flat sail instantly eased up into an easy bag and the boat walked right away from her rival. In light airs when the boat does not go through the water fast enough to make any appreciable amount of waves the principal resistance is the friction between the surface of the

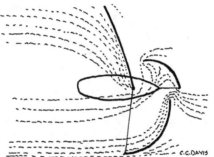

but - if mainsail and spinnaker are set so they form a funnel - live wind flows against them and also fills the baloon jib.

Fig. 34

boat and the water. Here is where a smooth polished bottom paint comes in and the boat with the most sail area in relation to the wetted surface of the bottom has the advantage.

Sailing a boat to leeward used to be considered the easiest point of sailing, but when a man has mastered the fine points of the game he learns that getting the yacht to leeward, instead, of being simple, is the most difficult, and calls for more skill and vigilance than when beating to windward.

You may think "Why even a leaf can blow along before the wind;" which is true enough, but racing puts a different value on the point. Another leaf may drift just as fast—now how are you going to make your leaf beat the other?

It used to be customary in running before the wind to square the mainboom off and set the spinnaker off the other side in line with it—as it was argued, in that position, the greatest possible area was exposed for the wind to act upon.

But wind is a fickle element and it was not understood by many who should have known more of its actions.

If you stand in front of a board fence, for instance, or the side of a building, with the wind blowing squarely against its surface, you do not feel the full force of the wind. Going around the corner it will lift you off your feet; the wind there forms a swift live current of air. Where you stood directly in front of the building, Fig. 32, a wedge-shaped volume of dead air was being pressed upon by the moving air, which divided some distance from the wall and flowed around the sides of the building. That is just the way the wind acted and still acts on a mainsail and spinnaker when both are set in a line square across the boat, Fig. 33. The "live" wind, as we call the air in motion, flows out around both edges; but if these two sails are set so they form a funnel, Fig. 34, and make all this live wind flow in a swift current between them, the pressure on each sail is not only increased but the balloon jib, that formerly hung limp and useless, is made to pull as hard as any.

Many a time when there seems to be no air moving when running before the wind, a slight luff will immediately produce a draft, and if you can so fill your sails and get headway on your boat you will find you can sail her down to leeward in two long zigzag legs or reaches and get there faster than if you drifted before it.

Relation of Spars to Shape of Sail

THE charm of sailing is the flexibility of all the component parts of a boat. The novice, learning only the first principles of sailing, sees only a few simple theories; but the more he learns about the sport, the more he will see there is yet to learn.

The boat itself is apparently subjected to whims, the spars and rigging are like banjo strings, all requiring tuning up to the proper tension to give the best results, and the sails are a soft, pliable cloth that can be maltreated or skilfully handled, according to the experience of the man in charge of them.

Add to all this the fact that the winds and waves are ever varying and what looks at first like a very simple problem one begins to realize is really a sport that will keep a man studying for some years. Then again, every type of boat has peculiarities of its own and every change in size produces an entirely different set of conditions, to anticipate which one must, like a physican, understand the underlying principles of boats.

I am not enumerating all these conditions to scare the novice, for the first rudiments—enough to sail a boat— are very simple; but have done so to show the man who takes to this sport what an endless variety of fine points he has to expand upon.

A great many sports are like a single musical instrument, while yacht racing is a whole orchestra.

Experience is the best teacher, but some pupils, quick to see, quick to hear, to move and to analyze cause and effect, will learn much more rapidly than others. That is where the personal element enters in. Takes a one-design class of boats, for instance—why does one man beat another in sailing his boat when both are just alike? Some men grasp the idea quicker; then again, there have been men who for a year or more have come in last nearly every race—now they are coming in winners, or up with the winners every time.

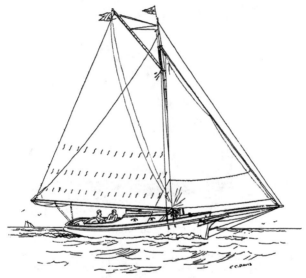

An Old-Time Cruiser

They were slower to pick up the idea of handling their boats, but none the less sure when they did. A great many people like to sail a boat, but lack confidence in themselves when it comes to racing. It is just this close competition which racing gives that puts the fine edge on a man's experience. He might sail about for years cruising by himself and never meet with one-half of the conditions that can arise in one yacht race. How much more instructive then is racing?

As an illustration of this, watch a dozen different men start in a race and see how some, judging their boat's speed against the moving second-hand of a watch and the

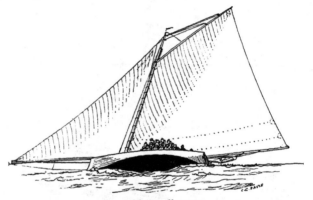

An Old Sandbagger

distance to the starting line, bring their boats across the line just as the starting signal is given—within a few seconds—and then see how slow others are to do the same thing. What better training can a man have in learning to sail a boat? None.

A man who goes through the training such a race gives him acquires skill and judgment that allows him to round up to a mooring in perfect confidence, while this is looked upon as a most difficult manœuver by the man who never has raced.

We all of us like to go away occasionally on a cruise, to jog along wherever one's fancy dictates, making a harbor of whichever port is easiest to reach, or go sailing along all night, under a big bright moon, for the novelty of it. When it breezes up fresh, isn't it glorious to carry on sail and feel your boat, which seems almost human as it bounds along, gather speed as you crack on the balloon jib! You enjoy the speed, the flying spray, the

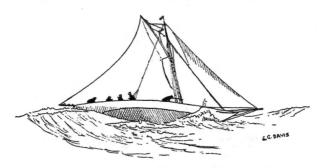

She Gathers Speed as You Crack on the Light Sails

roar under the lee low and the white, eddying wake astern. It's a pleasure to watch her speed increase as you adjust the trim of her sails so they pull to the very best advantage.

In a yacht race you have even a better chance to try the trim of your sails, for close alongside of you is a rival, also doing his best to make his boat go as fast as she can be made to.

Every alteration you make then in the set of your

sails or trim of your sheets, is made apparent as to whether it has helped or hindered the speed of your boat, for the other boat, like a thermometer, soon shows the result; she falls behind if the change is for the better, or *vice versa*.

Take a modern sloop as an illustration. If we were going to race this boat, the first thing is to see that she is in good condition. One of the most important things of all is to have a smooth, clean bottom. If she is a new

One of the Early Fin Keel Sloops

boat, the swelling of the wood squeezes the putty so it sticks out in ridges—she has "split her putty," as sailors say, and this offers considerable resistance to the passage of the hull through the water. She should have been hauled out or else landed on the beach at high water and when left high and dry, had her seams all scraped off smooth.

A great many men make the mistake of putting on fresh paint the day before the race. While this makes her look nice, it is detrimental to her speed. Fresh paint causes the water to cling to it, as if it were sticky. Lean over the side and watch how, when the boat rolls, a film of water is dragged up by the boat. It will make a far better racing bottom if the underbody, and top-sides, too, for that matter, had been rubbed and polished with very fine sandpaper. The old paint was hard, and this rubbing would have given it a hard smooth surface, which is what is needed. "Paint between races and polish before races" is advice worth remembering.

The next most important thing is to see that the spars and gear are all in first-class order. You can't expect the sails to set well if the spars bend so they let the sails sag out of shape. This can be corrected in many cases by shifting the bridles so the spars are held where the greatest strain comes.

Many gaffs are corrected in this way by shifting the peak halyard bridle out or in on the gaff. The mast, however, is the principal spar to look out for. There is a very heavy strain put upon the jibstay when the mainsail is trimmed down hard in beating to windward. Even wire rope stretches under such a strain, and this stretch allows the mast to tip back. This shifts the whole sail plan aft, and the boat is apt to gripe and carry a hard weather helm.

By tightening up this stay—and you want to watch the bobstay that holds the bowsprit down, as that, too, is apt to stretch—this hard helm can be corrected. You don't have to cut the wire and re-splice it; simply twist it up and this will shorten the length of the stay. See also that the mast stands straight and plumb, and is not pulled over to one side more than another.

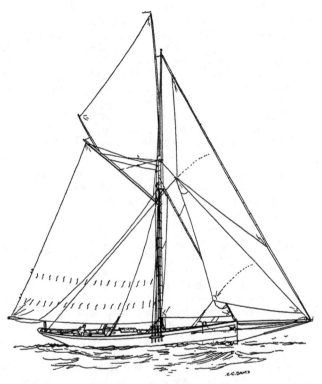

Type of British Cutter

The use of turnbuckles has made it so easy to set up the shrouds many men are doing so who are not competent to do so. They take up too much slack on one side— or they screw the mast down through the bottom of the boat. That is, they take up every particle of slack on both sides instead of allowing the shrouds to have some little slack, so the spar takes part of the strain. The deeper and narrower the boat, the tighter the shrouds can be—but wide, shallow boats should be given a little slack. Go carefully over all the ropes and pulleys and see that none of them is defective; many a race has been lost for want of a little attention of this sort.

Now we come to the sails, the most important of all, as they are the sole propelling power the boat has, and upon their condition all depends.

The hoisting of the sails may seem a very simple matter, but it is not so simple as it looks. In a very light air of wind they should not be hove up too tight; much greater speed can often be coaxed out of a yacht when the breeze dies down by slacking down on the halyards, so the sail hangs limp and loose. But if it is blowing hard, it is difficult to keep the sails from bagging and they should then be jigged up as hard as they will go.

For real hard racing rope halyards are tabooed. Rope stretches too much and shrinks so when wet or damp that you cannot depend upon them to hold the sails up as wanted, and in a close race you have no time to stop and swig them up.

Flexible steel wire rope is best, and in a boat of any size have a hauling end and a jib end as well. There is generally a great deal of difficulty experienced in keeping the throat of a sail hoisted, as the hoisting of the peak throws a heavy down-thrust on the gaff and that spar acts more or less as a pry to stretch the throat halyards. To jig up the throat when in a race is almost impossible. Realizing this, there has been a mainboom gooseneck invented, arranged with a spring that serves to keep the hoist tight. On the old, loose-footed mainsails on English cutters this was overcome by the use of a tack-tackle, but this arrangement is impractical with a mainsail that is laced to the boom. On a jib, however, that is the proper scheme. To hoist the jib on a wire halyard and then tack it down at the bowsprit or at the stem if she is a modern raceabout type with no bowsprit, by means of a wire pennant and single whip purchase.

Thirty-Foot Racing Sloop

You can get purchase enough in this way to pull the masthead clear forward so it slacks the jibstay, while the old way, where the jib has a permanent tack, it is sometimes impossible in a breeze to even tighten the jib sufficiently to prevent its sagging between the jib hanks.

A common fault in hoisting the mainsail is in not getting the peak up high enough. As the boat lays head to the wind at her moorings, the peak should be set up so a line of wrinkles shows from peak to tack. You will be surprised to see how quickly the apparent fullness disappears as soon as you fill away and start to sail. If she has rope halyards this will be particularly noticeable, and before starting in a race it will, more than likely, be necessary to luff her up into the wind and jig up again on both halyards.

A sail not peaked up enough is a most miserable-

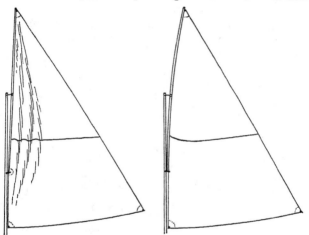

Sail Properly Hoisted and the way It Sets When the Wind Fills It

shaped piece of cloth to try and get any speed out of a boat with, either reaching or beating to windward.

There used to be a great deal of controversy over the merits of a curved surface or a perfectly flat surface for a sail, but aeroplanes have tested this out to the undeniable advantage of the curved surface.

But the exact shape of this curve is of equal importance; it should be a parabolic curve, the greatest depth of which from a straight line between mast and leech being about one-quarter the distance from the mast and the depth of the curvature in the sail about one-fifteenth of the width across the sail. The wind's action on such a curve (Fig. 35) gives a greater forward thrust than on either a true arc (Fig. 36) or a reversed parabolic curve (Fig. 37). An aeroplane that has wing surfaces as in Fig. 36 would drop straight down while one shaped like Fig. 37 would actually go backwards.

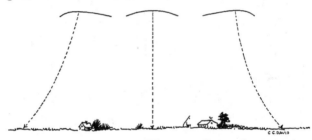

Action of an Aeroplane Wing Dropping to the Ground

Sailmakers, yacht designers and experienced yachtsmen had figured this curve out their own way years before scientists began to experiment with flying machines.

But in yachting, as in every other sport, new men come and the old men go, and what the old men have learned by a life-long study of boats generally dies with them; the new, younger men have to pick up their knowledge piece by piece, just as those old men did.

Some of their experience is rendered obsolete owing to

the radical changes made from time to time in the yacht's model. The trick, for instance, of luffing an old skimming-dish sandbag jib and mainsail boat out of a bad squall is of no use aboard a modern fin-keel canoe-shaped racer, but even then all is not lost, for the confidence one gets in his ability after a training under such conditions is valuable.

The methods employed in trimming sail on the two types of boats, however, are radically different. On the sandbagger the man at the "stick," as the tiller was

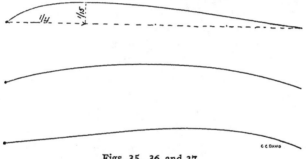

Figs. 35, 36 and 37

called, gave her a luff; the jib-sheet tender slacked off the lee sheet, "flowed his jib," to relieve the pressure on the big jib and assist the mainsail aft in turning the boat's head up toward the wind as a weather vane would turn. The sails were such immense pieces of cloth on those boats the helmsman relied as much on the quick action of his sail trimmers or sheet tenders to get speed out of the boat and keep her on her feet as he did on the helm; but on a modern fin-keeler, instead of having a

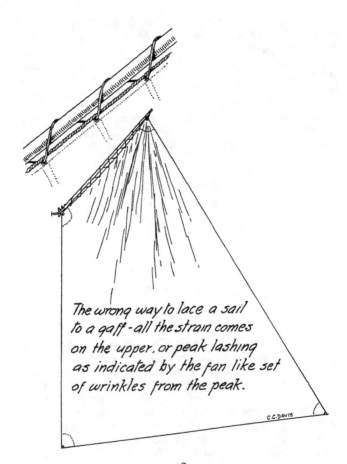

The wrong way to lace a sail to a gaff - all the strain comes on the upper, or peak lashing as indicated by the fan like set of wrinkles from the peak.

C. C. DAVIS

118

crew of about eight or ten men, counting sandbag slingers, sheet tenders and all, only about two men are carried. Such boats cannot capsize; they have a sinker of lead weighing tons hung well down under the boat on a thin fin of wood or bronze. They simply sit low down in the cockpit out of the wind and let her lay down to the puffs, the weight of the keel weighing out automatically the weight of the wind on the sails, and the hull is so shaped that even when heeled clear over on one edge

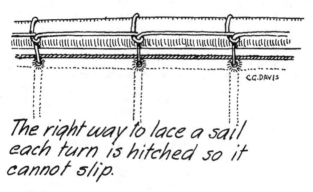

C.G.DAVIS

The right way to lace a sail each turn is hitched so it cannot slip.

she still has an easy canoe-shaped form in the water that glides ahead without a hand touching the main or jib sheets. The man at the tiller has the sole guidance of the ship in his hands.

With flush decks and small, narrow, bathtub-like cockpit, such boats cannot swamp or sink, but generally carry away their mast, rigging or sails; but the poor old jib and mainsail sandbagger—look at what he was up against! If the puff hit him too suddenly to turn his boat up into the wind, so he could luff through the squall, he could not very well luff when the lee deck edge was under water, for the reason that the stern is the part of the boat that swings when the rudder is turned, and to try to swing her stern around when its lee edge was under tended to cut it down deeper into the water and swamp her, for those boats had wide, open cockpits. It is one of the most ticklish moments and largely up to the sheet trimmers as well as the man at the stick to get her up into the wind a point or two and not bury the lee coaming. Many a sandbagger has come staggering out of such a squall with several barrels of water shipped over her lee coaming.

Such boats, however, bred sailors, for they carried a gang of men, not only one or two, as the boats of today do, but ten or twenty men, and there were more people per boat—friends of these men as spectators interested in watching the races as a consequence. On the other hand, we have ten or twenty yachts now, where there used to be one—and the sport is still growing.

To come back to the subject of sails. Many a first-class sail has been injured, if not ruined, by abuse in the way it is attached to the spars, and inefficiency in the spars to carry the sail properly.

Let me cite a few of these instances to you. A brand-new sail, for instance, is to be bent on for a race—maybe you think the fact that it is brand-new is an advantage—it is, just as a new pair of shoes are a comfort to the wearer. Why? For the very same reason the new shoes are a torture, generally, and that is their newness; they have not been stretched sufficiently to take out any of that natural elasticity which any new object has.

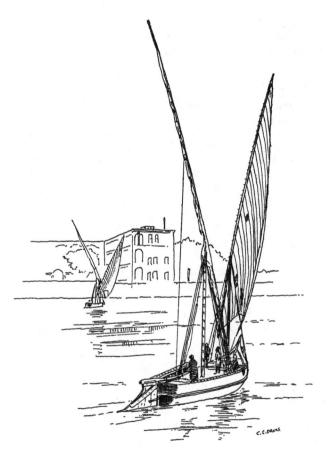

C.C.DAVIS.

121

If it should so happen that the first race was sailed in a nice light breeze, the new sail is the best you could have, but if it should come on to blow hard, the new sail, as sailors say, "would go all to pieces," which doesn't mean it would tear, but that the natural elasticity would be unduly pulled out locally; the four corners would be stretched in excess of the body of the canvas. This is what you don't want, and is the most common error made in bending a new sail. So common, that sailmakers generally attach a tag to the head and foot of each sail telling how far it should be stretched, and cautioning against stretching it any farther. Some inexperienced men used to put a tackle on the head and foot of a sail and make it come out to the end of the gaff and boom, points it should not stretch to for a month or more. Only haul a new sail out "hand taut," as they say, and little by little; as the whole sail stretches, just take up enough along the gaff and boom to smooth out any slack cloth that appears.

Many yachtsmen, rather then stretch a new sail in a hard breeze, withdraw from a race, and few will ever reef a brand-new sail, as it pulls the sail out of shape. If it has to be done, however, the sail will generally stretch itself back into shape in time.

More harm can be done a new sail than reefing it by not properly bending it onto the gaff. Not lacing it on with a rolling hitch or running hitch, which holds the sail firmly at each grommet as it should, but lacing it around and around, so the greatest stretch and sag comes in the middle of the sail, and all the strain is put upon the upper outer clew lashing. This generally develops a fan-like set of wrinkles from the peak down through the upper part of the sail, the lacing not supporting the sail uniformly along the gaff as it should.

You very often see instances where this same sort of defect is produced at the tack, owing to the clew of the sail being shackled into a part of the boom gooseneck too close in to the mast to correspond to the distance the mast hoops allow the sail to set away from the mast.

To preserve the springiness of "life," as it is called, of a new sail, the outer lashing on the gaff and boom should be slacked up after each race. On the boom, where it is more practical to do so than on the gaff, and where a greater body of the sail cloth is affected, a brass track is generally fitted along the top of the boom and the sail seized to brass slides that work in and out on this track, of which there are about a dozen different varieties.

The clew is fitted to haul out by means of a wire pennant rove over a sheave in the outer end of the boom, and either attached direct to the clew or more generally to a bronze casting that also slides on this track and extends the sail to the extreme end of the boom, for on a racing yacht every inch included in the measurement must be made use of. On very small yachts I have found it a still better practice to fasten the outer ends of the sail to the gaff and boom and then do the slacking up and hauling out from the inboard end, where it is much more get-at-able. Another reason for so doing is that in a one-design class, where all the boats have exactly the same sail area, by this means you are making use of the whole area it is possible to spread on the spars given. You can slack up your sails right from the mast and do not have to monkey around in a rowboat trying to come up with a wet, swollen peak or clew lashing.

On larger boats, the boom outhaul is by far the more shipshape rig of the two; if the mainsail be slightly damp and then begins to dry out and stretch, this slackness can be pulled out with such a purchase and outhaul at any time. Should it be a dry day when the race started, and on account of no wind, the finish be delayed until along towards sundown, when the air begins to get damp, or should a shower come up suddenly, a sail with no means of slacking it up would be badly stretched as the moisture shrinks up the canvas. With an outhaul the tackle can be slacked up a few inches and the life of the sail preserved.

A sail-maker's bench.

Getting the Proper Set to the Sail

IF you will work as hard to preserve that bird's-wing-shaped curve in the sail as the sailmaker did to produce it, your boat will fly faster through the water for such care and attention.

Not properly peaking up the gaff allows the whole sail to hang loose, and while it is not particularly harmful going before the wind, on the wind it makes a slow boat, and harms the sail.

The strain is allowed to hang from the nock or throat of the sail to the end of the boom, stretching the canvas tight there and allowing the slack cloths along the after leech to bag out where it should be flat to let the wind escape off the after leech.

The draft of the sail, instead of being along the luff by the mast, is in the after leech, and the boat cannot go well to windward.

If, however, the peak halyard be set up taut enough to strain the cloths down to the tack, all the after cloths along the leech are stretched out flat and smooth and the draft, or bagginess, is where it belongs—up near the mast.

Not properly hoisting up the throat is harmful to a sail, as soon becomes apparent when it breezes up a bit. The sail bellies out into two distinct bags when peak and throat are both slack, as shown by the way the shadows fall across the sail in Fig. 38. Setting the peak up properly makes a far better sail out of it, and takes away that hard dividing ridge from throat to clew, and gives a sail with considerable draft to it, as in Fig. 39.

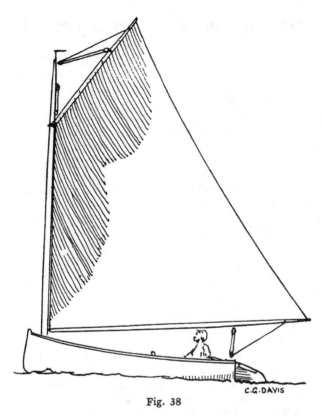

Fig. 38

As the breeze hardens, the slack cloth in the sail bulges out more than it should if the boat is to do her best close-hauled going to windward. Then jigging up tight on all the halyards will let her look up maybe half a point higher, and in looking at her sails end on, instead of bulging out as in Fig. 40, they will now stand

C.G.DAVIS

Fig. 39

like Fig. 41. The sail not swigged up good and hard cannot be properly sheeted down for windward work. The cloth of the sail is not stretched flat enough to hold the gaff in where it belongs—it will lay off to leeward and a good part of your sail is then not pushing to help her to windward with all the power it is capable of.

Remember this: swigging up tight on the sails is for hard winds. As the strength of the breeze moderates, so

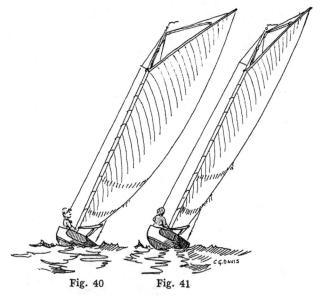

Fig. 40   Fig. 41

should the strain on the cloth be moderate by surging or slacking the halyards a trifle.

There is a great deal more headwork and good concentration in sailing a boat properly than most people are aware of.

The bending of the spars is in itself a study that

some men understanding it have used to advantage, while others have lost races through not studying it. It is easiest seen in the boom. If you will go up near the

Section through sail

Fig. 42

mast and sight along that spar, foreshortening it, you will be surprised to see how bent it really is; yet when looking at it sideways it appears perfectly straight. That bend affects your sail and perhaps the mast and gaff are bending just as badly. Only sailors don't call it bending; they call it "buckling."

Take a catboat as an example. I will have to exaggerate the points in view in order to make them plain. In light airs her spars all stand in straight lines, and her sails, cut to fit straight lines, sets nicely, as in Fig. 42.

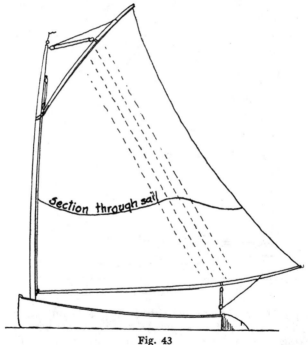

section through sail

Fig. 43

Now, in a hard breeze, what happens? Her mast bends some, the peak halyards pull the masthead aft, the push on the jaws of the gaff bend the mast forward, or try to, and the mainsheet pulled down hard tends to bend the whole mast from the deck up, as in Fig. 43. If the masthead comes back a foot, the peak must come back also; the gaff also bends, arched like a bow, and the end

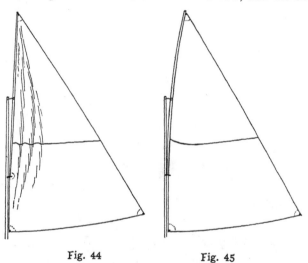

Fig. 44   Fig. 45

of the mainboom, held at the sheet strop, bends up on the end. Can't you imagine what happens to a sail under such conditions? The sail was never cut to such a shape and as a consequence the cloths shown dotted in Fig. 43 are stretched tight and the after cloths are all slack; so a section drawn across it showing its surface, or draft, becomes as shown in Fig. 43.

Many sails are spoiled by this defect, but experience

C.G.DAVIS

The Bend of the Mast is Controlled by the Headstay

has come to the rescue, and knowing about how much the local builders allow their boat's spars to bend, the sail-makers have so cut their sails that they will just come out nice and flat when the spars are bent, and in consequence, in a light air of wind the sails have excessive bagginess, or draft. They cut the sweep or "roaches" on the edges of the sails so the sails will not pull tight in one spot but flatten all over as it breezes up.

In the sliding gunter rig, or the standing lugsail, used extensively on small yachts in English waters, the bend of the gaff or yard is made to serve a good purpose. The sail is cut with considerable fullness along the luff or yard, as shown in Fig. 44, by the shaded wrinkles.

This, in light winds, before the yard is bent any, throws a bag or draft in the luff of the sail. As soon as the breeze hardens, the strain bends the yard so it pulls this slack cloth in the luff tighter, and by careful study in cutting the proper curve and in getting a yard to bend true, the sail becomes flatter and flatter the harder it blows—just what is desirable for the speed of the boat. As the after leech is moved aft by the tip of the yard bending aft, the whole sail is pulled out flatter, as in Fig. 45. Experience in the setting of sails, as in any other game, comes to those who study and analyze cause and effect. If his yacht's spars bend, a seasoned yachtsman would either shift the pulleys or, by wire bridles, bring the strain on a different point of the spar.

One of the Cup defenders had a mainboom trussed with struts and wire guys to prevent its bending. The strut and strut-stay down the front of a racing sloop's mast to counteract the thrust of the jaws of the gaff are a common sight in yachts of today, while in Europe, the Marconi, or wireless mast, as it is nicknamed, is fast coming into favor.

The success of the tall leg-o-mutton sail carried on

133

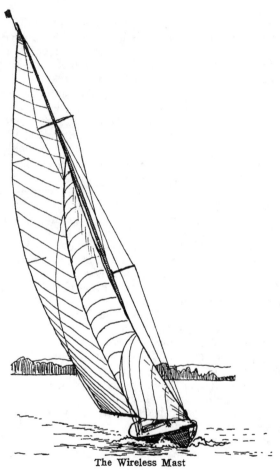

The Wireless Mast

134

this mast, strangely enough, depends as much on the headstay as it does on the shrouds or side stays. By slacking or tightening this headstay, the long fishpole-like mast is under absolute control and the efficiency of the sail in light or heavy weather regulated largely by its manipulation.

Storing Sails

T HE care that sails receive has a great deal to do with how long they will last. A suit of sails left, as we often see them on small boats, rolled up indifferently, collecting puddles of water in their folds every time it rains—which either stays there until it is evaporated by the sun and wind or at least long enough before the sail is again used to start decay in the fibre of the cloth—left entirely uncovered or what is even worse, covered with a torn or improper canvas covering which lets water in on the sail and then, like the lid on a pot on the stove, it keeps the heat and moisture in the sail, such sails will last but a short time.

Good sails deserve good care and so do any sails that you expect to get good work out of. Never, for instance, roll up wet sails into a snug furl and put a sail cover on. It may be at the end of a day's sail, or the end of a wet race, but if too late in the evening to dry the sails, just roll them up loosely, leave the sail cover off and hoist them up to dry next morning, as soon as the sun's warmth begins to be felt. The trouble here is that many men have to be at business the next day and while some have the club janitor or boatman, who will see that the sails are properly dried, some have no one to look after their boat. Where this is the case, the sails are bound to deteriorate.

New canvas has more or less sizing or starchy substance in its fibre; this starch decays and forms small spots of discoloration that spreads in time until the canvas is no longer white. Where soft coal soot permeates the atmosphere that, too, soon discolors a sail, but while it is not beautiful to look at, it does not have the injurious effect that the mildew has. Mildew is decomposition, while coal dust simply stains.

It is to ward off the mildew that new sails are sometimes put through a mildew-proof process or pickling. This soaking them in a bath that removes the starchy substance and fills the fibre of the canvas with a substitute which is not affected by the weather prolongs their life. Fishermen sometimes tan their sails to prevent mildew. See that the canvas is drying when furling the sails. Roll them up into a snug furl, using gaskets or ties of canvas folded two or three thicknesses into flat narrow bands that do not cut the canvas as a hard rope is apt to when pulled hard against a bight or fold in the sail, and put a waterproof sail cover over it. A sail so stowed will go through showers during the week, when the yacht's owner is attending to business, and be in good shape when hoisted for the Saturday and Sunday sailing.

An extra good racing sail might better be unbent and taken ashore where it can be kept dry and clean—and this practice you will find largely in vogue among racing yachtsmen. Light brass tracks are screwed fast to the underside of the gaff and the top of the boom with small specially made "hanks" lashed to the head and foot of the sail which enables the sail to be quickly slipped on or off the spars, as soon as the cringle lashings are let go.

If you had a sail bag made when you had the mainsail made, put it into this bag every time you unbend it and so keep it clean. If you have no sail bag get some old canvas and after folding your sail up into a snug bundle, roll it up in this canvas and tie it up securely or better yet, take palm, sail needle and twine and sew it up so tightly no mice can get into the folds to make a nest. If they do they are apt to gnaw a hole in the new sail to make a cotton-down lined nest.

To the average man who cannot afford a new suit of sails every Spring, the preservation of a good suit over the Winter means a great deal.

A new suit of sails rolled up while still damp or stored in a damp place will be so rotted with mildew that more often than not they won't last the season out.

There are a few things which should be looked after when storing them away. First of all they should be thoroughly dried. This may either be done before un-bending the sail by hoisting it about three-quarters of the way up and letting the sun and wind dry it, or it may be removed and spread out on the dry grass, turning it over after a while so that the sun has a chance to shine on both sides.

Should it so happen that the sail has been wet, say along the foot, it would be well to wash the salt out with fresh water.

If the sail is dirty and it is desired to clean it before storing away, the following is a very fine bleach, and is not injurious to the canvas if well washed out:

         Washing Soda .... 1½ lb
         Chlorinated Lime 2   lb
         Water .... 2½ gallons

Put them together a day or two before required and stir occasionally. Lay the sail out on a gravel beach or other clean place, wet it with water (clean salt water will do) and with a scrubbing brush go all over the sail with the above mixture. After an hour or so wash the sail out well with fresh water and dry in the sun.

In putting the sail away in a locker make sure that it is a dry one, and that the roof doesn't leak. Instead of putting it at the botom of all your equipment, build a rack near the ceiling where you are sure it won't lay in any possible puddles.

In rolling up a sail to store away, do not see into how small a bundle you can make it, but fold it loosely and tie it so that you can handle it easily.

And last, when it has been put away, it is a very good plan to throw a light piece of material over it to keep off any dust that may settle on it.

If there are any repairs to be made, don't wait until the Spring, when the first warm breeze blows. Do it now. It will insure getting repairs made when the shops are not piled up with work and everyone at fever heat. It also helps the sailmakers, in that they will have something for their crews, or hands, to work at, when otherwise they would be idle.

Racing Kinks

Making a Yacht Do Her Best

SOME people think sailing a boat is the same in all cases. You get aboard, hoist sail, let out the sails if the wind is fair or pull them in close if it be ahead and the boat glides along on the water.

Now this is just as true as driving a horse consists of sitting in a carriage holding the reins in your hands and pulling the rein on the side to which you want the horse to turn.

If it is a blind horse, or a steady-going old family skate that will shy at nothing and could not run faster than a dog trot if it tried, such handling will answer, but suppose the horse is a little spirited and gets up on his hind legs when an automobile whizzes by or takes a side jump, which rein are you going to pull? Neither. It's then a case of master mind, telegraphed by certain feelings on the reins to the horse, that a superior being sits in control of him, that guides the horse's actions. He feels it and while he might bolt with an unexperienced driver a good whip will hold him right down on his four feet.

Boats are the same way, that is racing boats, yachts of some ability and high strung like the spirited horse. They require just as much jockeying and feeling of positive control on their tillers. If anything the yacht game is more keen for it is the result of the helmsman's own skill in anticipating various moves that makes her jump ahead and take every advantage of the wind. Only a fractional difference in trim or point of sailing may exist, but it's that small fraction that makes the difference between losing or winning a race and it takes experience to acquire the judgment to decide that frictional difference.

Some things can be verbally explained, and by accompanying motions of hands or fingers, that look ridiculous to one not hearing the conversation, express by a single

A 6-Foot Australian Racer

move to your companion more than it would require a whole sentence to write out.

It is so in this case, but even with the handicap of cold type we'll go into the subject of boat-sailing.

The foundation of all knowledge is experience—so get all you can. I may often refer to the particular event when certain knowledge came to me. Don't think me egotistical if I refer to it; we will get at the gist of the subject all the quicker so, than if I try to hide my personality behind the book cover by referring to an unknown second or third person.

There are two views of the sport of racing sailing yachts. One is the view of the yachtsman whose aim is to accumulate the most number of prizes purely for the miserly spirit of getting all he can by sailing or by protesting, fair means or foul, that he may display them to substantiate his brag of his skill; the other is that view taken by the true sportsman who races for the pure love of sailing—who would just as soon race if there were no prizes—who races for the experience it gives him and the consequent skill attained in handling a sailboat in a greater variety of circumstances than ordinary day sailing could give.

Every race is a mimic battle as it were—each presenting different conditions of wind and water and a variety of manœuvers, due to the varying conditions bound to arise when several boats are all aiming to cross the line, as in a start, at the same place, at the same time, that give a yachtsman such a training as he can get in no other way.

The fact that it is a competition puts a keen interest into the sport that has appealed to the better spirits of sporting men and year by year the sport has gradually grown to its present popularity, one hundred and eight boats starting in one race at Larchmont, N. Y.

STUDY THE COURSE

Tide.—Familiarity with the course over which the yacht is to sail is a great advantage and often the cause of a boat's winning the race.

Realizing this the racing instructions now generally include a printed chart with the course ruled on it so strangers may see just where they are supposed to go.

But even with such a chart before one, with a compass on the boat, which many small yachts do not have, the man so familiar with the course that he knows just where each mark is at a glance has an advantage. It isn't necessary for him to look at his compass, he knows the buoy they are to turn is just under a high tree that stands out conspicuously on the distant shore line, or just to the right of a clearing in the trees that shows up a bald, grassy lawn. If one has the time it would pay him to go out and sail around the course and get the bearings in mind for each mark he will have to turn.

Have you ever on a rainy day watched the rain-water as it flows along the gutter—how it forms eddies behind obstructions, how it flows as rapids over shallow places and all such antics the water goes through? If you haven't, do so, and think why the water does as you see it. If you have you will realize that it is the shape of the shore and the character of the bottom over which the water flows that causes tide rips and eddies and you will be quicker to realize what the surface water indicates and make use of favorable eddies and avoid unfavorable ones.

We all know that water forms an eddy back of any obstruction placed in a stream of swift flowing water, but a man is not apt to consider an island six miles long as a pebble in the gutter, yet with a strong flood tide running we had a clear demonstration one Summer that there is just such an eddy formed behind such an island.

In this case we were anchored in the middle of the Race at the eastern end of Long Island Sound with a strong flood tide just starting to run. We were trying to get to Sarah's Ledge in New London Harbor to the north of us.

All night long we had come down the Sound racing in Whileaway against three other schooners from Stamford. After a while a light breeze struck up from the south'ard, we got underway before it, setting our spinnaker, but the way that tide set us westward back up the Sound was discouraging. We could see land slipping along back of the Bartlett Reef lightship as if that ship were steaming to the eastward.

We were about three miles away from Fisher's Island when I suddenly noticed we had stopped drifting sideways and that the lightship was no longer slipping by the land. I realized in a moment we were in an eddy formed behind Fisher's Island so took in our spinnaker and with a four or five-mile tide running west just outside of us to the southward we went sailing east in a fair eddy until close up to the island, when we squared away again and ran in before the wind to the finish line and won the race.

Now who would compare Fisher's Island to a pebble in the gutter, yet you see the water acts the same in both cases!

Another instance when I learned how water eddies behind a point of land was away back in 1896. We had rounded Matinicock Point buoy, the last boat in the fleet, and there was a string of boats stretched out a couple of miles ahead of us beating back to City Island all standing north on the port tack. From our position astern of the Ellsworths' Mary II, I noticed the line of boats sagged off, the leader, Sasqua, being carried off to leeward by the strong ebb tide sweeping around Sands Point and out the Sound. So we came about, stood close up under the Long Island shore where, as we found out afterwards, we had a fair eddy helping us along. The result was we were so far ahead of the rest of our rivals that, while our cat was in the twenty-five-foot class we finished right with the two big thirty-foot cats, Molly Bawn and Weasel, and at first were accused of not having gone over the course. It was certainly a startling example to me of what a help the current can be in a race.

The most astonishing demonstration in this line I ever saw was in the race from New Rochelle to Block Island when the small sloop Okee sailed all night with a breeze that put her down to her deck edge and followed every indentation along the Long Island beach about a hundred yards off shore in slack water most of the time while a whole fleet of larger boats lay becalmed with a head tide a little farther out off this shore. Okee won the race.

In sailing a race it often happens that the tide turns and begins to flow back just the opposite to what it has been running. This is one thing you want to watch and know just what time the turn takes place. It turns first along the shores and will often be running a strong flood along the beach while there is still a strong ebb tide running out in the deeper channel.

Owing to the fact that both sides of the points of land are not always the same, one side we will say being bold and deep along shore, while the other side is a shelving shallow, sandy beach, the direction in which the water is deflected from these points varies considerably and should be studied. Watch lobster floats, oyster stakes or boats at anchor and you can often see how the tide flows. Very often this knowledge can be used to good advantage. Sometimes it pays to "pinch a boat," that is, to sail her very close to the wind in order to place the boat in such an angle in reference to the direction the tide is setting as to cause this tide to press against the lee bow and shove the boat up to windward.

A Chesapeake Bay Bugeye

Winds.—While the flow and change of tides can be calculated to almost the minute, though a strong wind will often hold back or hasten the turning time, with winds the case is entirely different, and as sailing yachts rely on wind for their motive power, you can see the importance of judging this fickle element.

146

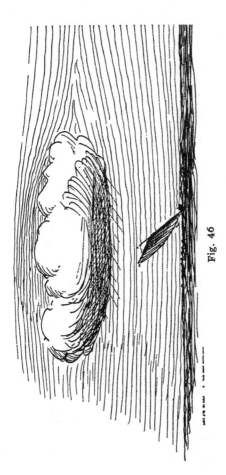

Fig. 46

147

In its action, although the eye cannot see it, wind behaves very much the same as water. It banks up in front of an obstruction, flows swiftly, like rapids around the corners and forms back eddies behind them just as water.

For this reason one must consider the land formation as that may deflect the wind somewhat and a knowledge of these local wind shifts is a decided advantage in sailing a race.

You probably have heard the saying "Every cloud has its puff of wind," and as the clouds scud by overhead the yacht does get a harder squall, but the wind does not come out of the cloud. Fig. 46.

Like a stone in the gutter obstructing the flow of water the cloud is an obstruction in the swiftly moving body of air, and the air sweeps under the cloud with increased velocity, just as the water in the gutter rushes through the congested opening past the sides of the stone.

In this paragraph and the next, the author shows ignorance of cloud physics. A cloud cannot obstruct or deflect the wind, as it is part of the wind. Just as a small volume of muddied water is part of the river, the cloud is part of the flow. The phenomenon he attributes to the cloud is actually what causes the cloud, an updraft that raises air to a greater altitude where the consequent cooling and pressure drop causes condensation, forming the cloud. As the air rises, other air flows in at the surface to take its place. Rather than the cloud causing the air flow, the air flow has created the cloud. The author describes this phenomenon at the bottom of page 149.

When the passing cloud is large enough to bank up a large part of the air above the water, leaving only a narrow space between it and the water, we have a squall. The rapid rush of air under this cloud is accentuated owing to the narrowness of the space through which the air has to pass. Fig. 47.

The exact intensity of a squall is a thing it is almost impossible to foretell. The barometer, a delicate instrument for weighing the density of the air, is the best guide we have; but that, while it shows any sudden changes in the weight of the atmosphere due to heat or cold, wetness or dryness, is of no value in foretelling the speed with which the wind is going to travel during the squall—it does show that a change is coming and you have to judge the violence of the coming wind by the rapidity of the rise or fall as indicated by the mercury in the barometer.

Experience alone will teach you what to expect from a squall. Sometimes it gets so black before the squall you look for a fearful blast of wind and are agreeably disappointed; at other times it does not look so bad, but when the squall hits it is bad, far worse than you want it to be.

But outside of squalls, of which you may not get one all season, there are other tricks about the wind one should learn.

For instance, at the western end of Long Island Sound, when racing with the usual Summer southerly wind, we always look for the wind to haul around more to the westward as the sun gets around in the west, late in the afternoon. As we say, "The wind goes around with the sun," and we calculate accordingly when sailing a race.

Another peculiarity, which is easily explained, is the way in which a boat away off to leeward often seems to get the first air of wind after a dead calm has prevailed. We always explained it by saying the wind struck over our boat, but that is not strictly true.

A light air after a calm is caused by the air in some place becoming warm and consequently lighter than the

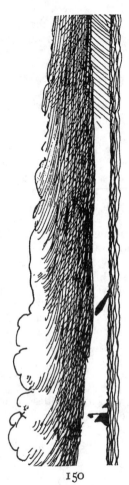

Fig. 47

surrounding air. As the warm air rises the cooler air flows in, is warmed also, and a current of uprising air started just as if a bonfire had been built—as at the point C in diagram 48.

It is the uprising of the air at C that draws the air towards this point; it is but natural therefore that the boat at A should be the first to feel this draught. It is some time later before the boat at B feels this slight draught, for we are speaking now of when it is an absolute calm. In other words, the air is not pushed in towards C, but is sucked in towards that point.

Another point is that as you approach the land the wind generally veers a little square to the shore.

Along the north shore of Long Island, with a southerly breeze, the wind will come off the beach at right angles to the shore and a boat can lay her course a rap full along the shore, while half a mile or more out in the Sound other boats are headed off and cannot point up within two points of where the boats in under the beach can.

I have already told you how the little Okee worked the land breeze, as we call it, and beat the whole fleet, big and little, in the Block Island race one year. This land breeze is caused by the difference in temperature between the water and the land, as the temperature of the land changes at sunset and sunrise. At sunset the land cools more quickly than the water and the cold, heavier air slides out and under the warmer air on the water, in the form of a night breeze. You see this everywhere along the seashore, when the sea breeze has blown all day; as night sets in this wind dies out and an offshore breeze blows for awhile. Fig. 49.

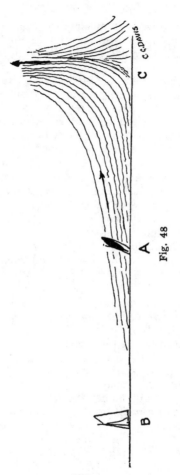

Fig. 48

In the morning, when the sun's heat again comes upon the scene, the water, like glass, reflects the sun's heat and the air over the water is warmed up first, again causing an unbalanced condition of the air. The warmed air rises and the cool land air moves out to fill the space as the hot air rises.

This is just as true on the Great Lakes as it is on salt water as I once had occasion to observe. We, on Psammaid, had rounded Detroit Light, in an all night race around the western end of Lake Erie. Two big sloops were ahead of us. It was a flat calm, but as dawn approached a faint air gave us steerageway and we let our boat run well in towards the shore, caught the new land breeze first; it didn't extend more than a mile off-shore, and in this fresh wind we ran up on the leaders and made up about two miles they had been ahead of us.

The clouds themselves often give an idea of where the wind is coming from; watch them and study their appearance.

Freak conditions will of course arise occasionally, and put your wits to the test. I remember one race when we all started from Larchmont on a broad reach with a very light westerly breeze; over near the Long Island shore the leading boat stopped becalmed. The next boat ranged up alongside of her and she stopped; one after another, about seven of us, all came to a dead stop, like a line of soldiers on parade. The only reason I could see for this was a low, straight cloud right up over the line of yachts. In some way that cloud produced an eddy and the westerly breeze stopped dead at that point. Seeing the others all stop, we hauled up and took our place in the southern end of the line. A southerly striking in

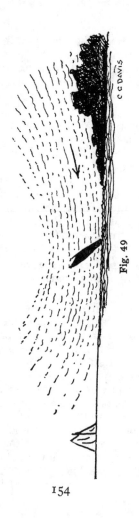

C C DAVIS

Fig. 49

soon afterwards gave us the weather gauge on our rivals.

Another day I was sailing up along the New York shore beyond Milton Point with a stiff puffy nor'west wind blowing, when all of a sudden the main boom jibed over. I rolled my wheel down; the Freyja luffed around a complete circle and then went on east with the same nor'west wind. A regular little whirlpool in the air had hit us. The funny part of this is, I was telling a yachtsman friend of mine of this experience one day several years later when he told me he had had the same experience in the same place. Some formation in the land evidently produced this whirling eddy when the wind was in the right direction.

In September 8, 1906, in the Manhasset Bay Yacht Club Regatta sailed on Long Island Sound, another freak wind was experienced. A stiff nor'easter had been blowing all morning and was blowing when the New York Yacht Club one-design thirty-footers started. Hardly had they gone when the wind began to veer around to the westward, although where they were the wind stayed northeast. Off to the southward we could see big coasters coming out past City Island with a stiff southwester. The Class P boats started, then the Class T and when the Q's started they had the wind dead aft from the west and set spinnakers, and five minutes later when we started this southwester had just hit us, and away we went on the starboard tack. At this time the boats under the New York shore were heeled decks to on the port tack. The Q's and other boats lay becalmed after running before the wind a couple of miles in the middle of the Sound and we in the handicap class to the southward within a couple of hundred yards of them were running east decks to on the starboard tack. These two distinct winds continued until the two divisions of boats almost came together on opposite tacks off Milton Point when the southerly wind prevailed and then all proceeded on the starboard tack. But such freak winds are the exception.

On July 2, 1907, there was a remarkable sight in the finish of the Larchmont race, when about thirty small sloops all lined up as if on parade, due to the southerly wind banking up and stopping about a quarter of a mile from the finish line. All the tail-enders came along before the wind and caught up to boats that had left them a mile astern. As we all lay here wetting our fingers to try and feel an air of wind the big schooner yachts Queen and Ingomar came along under balloon sails, went through our fleet, their upper sails in a fine breeze, while low on the water our small sails could not feel a breadth of it.

Three days later, on July 25th, two boats, Naiad and Little Peter, were running neck and neck for the finish line in a light southerly air, when within a boat's length of the finish there came a single, solitary puff of wind dead ahead. Naiad's skipper saw it, dropped his spinnaker, trimmed in his sheets, and close-hauled, shot across the line, winner. Little Peter was caught aback, with her spinnaker set, lost her headway and, as a dead calm succeeded this single puff, it was ten minutes before she, too, finished. These illustrations will show the amateur yachtsman some of the peculiar freaks the air will perform at times, and for that reason, he must always be on the watch to see and take advantage of every little shift that occurs.

♆